Reformation & Revival

OTHER BOOKS *from* VISION FORUM

Reformation & Revival

THE STORY OF THE ENGLISH PURITANS

JOHN BROWN

Edited by Michael Gobart
Foreword by Douglas W. Phillips

THE VISION FORUM, INC.
SAN ANTONIO, TEXAS

ISBN-10 1-934554-32-4

ISBN-13 978-1-934554-32-6

Cover Design by Roger Hall
Typography by Peter J. Serven

10 9 8 7 6 5 4 3 2 1

PRINTED IN THE UNITED STATES

CONTENTS

FOREWORD

During the year 2009, the eyes of the world will turn to remember the anniversaries of the birth of the two most influential men of the last one thousand years. This year marks the 500th anniversary of the birth of John Calvin and the 200th anniversary of the birth of Charles Darwin. (It is also the 150th anniversary of the publication of Darwin's *magnum opus*, *The Origin of the Species*.)

No two men of the millennium have done more to shape the thoughts of mankind or to affect the political and social destiny of nations than Calvin and Darwin—the former for great good and the glory of God, and the later for unimaginable evil.

The book in your hand is an exploration of one critical

component of Calvin's legacy: the English Reformation and the rise of Puritanism in Great Britain. Concerning Darwin, the subject of his true spiritual, social, and political legacy must be left for consideration in other books, sermons, and treatises. Let it suffice for now to observe that Darwin—and the widespread acceptance of his Theory of Evolution as it has been applied to philosophy, science, economics, theology, and virtually every primary academic discipline—has sadly done more to undo the work of Calvin and the Reformers than any other single philosophical influence.

As to the contrast of the legacies of the two men, I will add only this: Where Calvin taught the inadequacies of the fallen mind of man, the supremacy of the law of God, and the sufficiency of Holy Scripture, Darwin's Theory led to the supremacy of man's autonomous reason, the rejection of Scripture as infallible and inerrant, and to widespread distrust in the Bible as an accurate record of Earth history. The children of Calvin and the Reformers gave us the rise of nation states that embraced Republican representative government. The children of Darwin gave us Marxism and totalitarianism. Calvin's legacy included respect for life, a defense of the biblical family, and the rule of law under God. Darwin's philosophical progeny introduced the world to the horrors of eugenics and legalized widespread abortion on demand. Where Calvin insisted that law was transcendent, being created by God for the good of man and as a reflection of His unchanging righteousness, the followers of Darwin would insist that laws evolve, that the Bible is non-applicable to matters of the state, and the transcendent standards of morality do not even exist. The reforms of Calvin resulted in the blossoming of Christendom. Darwin foreshadowed the darkness of modernity.

In sum, our world and the battles facing the Church today in many respects reflect the tension between the antithetical worldviews of these two men. And this is why for the quincentennial of Calvin's birthday it is critical that we become intimately familiar with those Reformers who shared his basic presuppositions and who inaugurated what many believe to be the high watermark of wisdom and spirituality in the modern history of the Church—Puritanism and the English Reformation.

This anniversary edition of John Brown's original volume *The Story of the English Puritans*, first published in 1910, is a succinct, helpful introduction to these remarkable men, their teachings, their battles, their martyrdoms, and the legacy of freedom in Christ purchased with their blood and bequeathed to future generations. Though the formal history of the English Puritans begins in the mid sixteenth century, the roots of this Reformation run deeper. They can clearly be found in the cause of the Bible-believing Waldenses of the twelfth century, in the fallout from the persecutions and papal supremacy declarations of the thirteenth century, and in the fourteenth century work of the great Bible translator John Wycliffe, the "Morning Star of the Reformation." We see more seeds of reformation planted when the Gutenburg Press arrives in 1450, thus allowing the widespread dissemination of God's Word to the masses. By the beginning of the sixteenth century, Martin Luther had nailed his 95 Theses to the door of the Wittenberg Chapel, and early martyrs of the Reformation would emerge in Great Britain including Hamilton, Wishart, Ridley, Latimer, Cranmer, and the great William Tyndale, whose final words on the stake were: "Lord open the eyes of the King of England." By the time that John Hooper, the father of Puritanism, and later Thomas Cartwright, the father of English Presbyterianism, would arrive on the scene in the 1560s and 70s respectively, much fertile spiritual ground had been tilled.

The far reaching influence of Puritanism exists to the present day, but the formal era of Puritanism lasted but one century—from the accession of Elizabeth to the throne in 1558, to the death of Cromwell in 1658. During that one hundred years, Christendom was blessed with some of her best works of literature, best theologies, and best confessions of faith in the history of the Church. It was an age of tremendous courage and vision.

In terms of the practical application of the Word of God to every area of life, no movement in Church history has been so prolific, so profound, and so potent. For the Puritans, the Bible was the only guide for faith and practice. The Bible required orthodoxy, but orthodoxy demanded orthopraxy—the practical outworking of the faith in the real world. It was the foundation of ethics, law, philosophy, business, and science. It spoke to contracts, recreation, child training, and warfare—in fact, there was nothing to which the Bible did not speak, at least in principle.

Better than any group in the previous thousand year history of the Church, the Puritans understood jurisdiction and the importance of sphere sovereignty. Consequently, the Puritans gave the world the most sophisticated, most practical, and most biblical understanding of the doctrine of the family in the history of the Church. They did the same for the doctrine of the church and the doctrine of the state.

It was the latter which paved the way for the American War for Independence. But for the Puritans, it is difficult to imagine that an intellectual consensus rooted in biblical principles of law and jurisdiction would have emerged as the theological foundation of American independence. Our republic was birthed in colonial teachings inherited from Calvin and the Puritan reformation about the priesthood of the believers, the transcendent nature of law, equality of the law, leadership by elders, and distinct jurisdictions of church and state—both under God.

Nicknamed by King George "A Presbyterian parson's rebellion," the American Republic was conceived in the pulpit as it was encouraged and justified by seventeenth century pastors who cut their teeth on Puritan writings like Samuel Rutherford's *Lex Rex* which provided a biblical defense of resistance against tyranny. It was Calvin and the English Puritan doctrines (not the democracy of the Greeks) which gave America a distinctively republican system of government.

The Fifth Commandment tells us to honor our fathers so that it will be well with us, and so that we will live long in the land given to us by God. As Americans who have drawn deeply from the rich heritage of the Reformers, it is appropriate that we take advantage of anniversary years like the Calvin quincentenniary to remember the faith of our fathers and to inquire into the worldview which inspired them. It is the aspiration of the publishers that this anniversary edition will help you to do just this.

Persevero,
DOUG PHILLIPS
Vision Forum, 2009

PREFACE

The work here presented to the reader is intended to give, within moderate compass and in the light of recent research, the history of the rise, growth and decline of that Puritan movement which, for a hundred years, so vitally affected the course of our national life. It aims at a middle course. There have been historical monographs dealing with separate portions of the movement; and there have also been connected histories of it as a whole; but the monographs were necessarily sectional and incomplete; and on the other hand the connected histories were too elaborate and therefore too lengthy for readers with only limited time at their disposal, but who yet wished to arrive at a fairly trustworthy knowledge of the subject. It is hoped this little book may to some extent meet the needs of readers of this class.

The subject is worthy of attention, for Puritanism had important bearings both upon the religious life and the constitutional history of the nation. It was first of all theological in character, being a call for both doctrinal and personal reformation. Secondarily, the theological foundations of Puritanism worked out to political results. Republican government under God is the child of the Reformation.

For in the Reformation the two levers used to break the authority of the Holy See were free enquiry and the priesthood of all believers; and these two principles contained in them the germs of the political revolution which has come to pass. For they made the community the visible centre of the Church, and the people the principal factor of social life. On these grounds the history of the English Puritans deserves to be known from within and in such connected form as the necessary limitations of space will allow.

J. B. HAMPSTEAD

June 20, 1910

CHAPTER I

The ORIGINS *of* PURITANISM

Puritanism, as a recognized descriptive term, came into use, Thomas Fuller tells us, about the year 1564. But as there were reformers before the Reformation, so there were Puritans before that which has come to be regarded as in a special sense the Puritan period. For Puritanism was not so much an organized system as a religious temper and a moral force, and being such it could enter into combinations and alliances of varied kind. It may fairly be applied to Wycliffe and the Lollards as well as to the later protestant reformers; to Hooper and Latimer in the days of Edward VI as well as to Cartwright and Travers in those of Elizabeth; to some who remained within the pale of the English Church and to others who separated from it. The name was not confined to Presbyterians and Congregationalists, for there were bishops who may be described as distinctly Puritan; nor was it to be identified with the Calvinistic system of doctrine, for Archbishop Whitgift, who was the most resolute opponent of the Puritans, was, as his Lambeth Articles show, a believer in predestination in its extremist form. The term came also to have a political as well as an ecclesiastical significance. While in the sixteenth century it was descriptive of the men bent on carrying on the protestant Reformation to a further point, in the seventeenth century it became the recognized name of that party in the State which contended for the constitutional rights and liberties of the people as against the encroachments of the Crown.

And even yet we have not enumerated all possible applications. What an old writer calls "this reproachful word Puritan," was applied scoffingly to men who were regarded as foolishly precise in the matter of forms and ceremonies; it was also applied seriously to some of the greatest names in our history and literature—to Cromwell and Milton, to Baxter and Bunyan. Then it was but a step from those who were thought to be needlessly precise as to forms of worship, to pass to men who were thought to be needlessly strict as to life and morals. Richard Baxter relates that his father was jeered at as a

Puritan, though a strict conformist to the Church and the Book of Common Prayer, because he read the Bible with his family on Sunday afternoons and refused to join in the merry-makings then going on round the maypole which stood by the great tree near his door. As was said by a writer of those days: "In the mouth of a drunkard he is a Puritan who refuseth his cups; in the mouth of a swearer he which feareth an oath; in the mouth of a libertine he who makes any scruple of common sins."

Still, while the name thus varied in its applications with time and persons and the course of events, we discern at once a common element of characteristic sort running through all the variations. The fundamental idea of Puritanism in all its manifestations was the supreme authority of Scripture brought to bear upon the conscience as opposed to an unenlightened reliance on the priesthood and the outward ordinances of the Church. The Puritan, whether narrow or broad, mistaken or enlightened, seemed, to himself at least, to be aiming, not at singularity, but at obedience to that higher spiritual order prevailing in the universe, which he recognized as being the expression of the mind of God, and therefore of more commanding authority than the mere arrangements and requirements of man. Under all its forms, reverence for Scripture, and for the sovereign majesty of God, a severe morality, popular sympathies and a fervent attachment to the cause of civil freedom have been the signs and tokens of the Puritan spirit.

While saying thus much we are not concerned to deny that there were Puritans who did not realize the greatness of their own idea. There were those among them who had not that wider conception of the action of the Spirit of God in human life which leads a man to regard scholarship, knowledge, art and beauty as sacred things; they may not have always heard the voice of God speaking through the forces of history and in the facts of daily life as well as from the pages of revelation; and they may not have sufficiently recognized the developments of man's richer nature as gifts of God, God's way of unfolding man himself, enriching his culture and sweetening his life. But this is only true in a narrow and limited sense. Both in the sixteenth and seventeenth centuries, the leaders of the Puritans were among the foremost of their age in learning and intellectual force. They were, for the most part, university men, and for culture and refinement of taste had no need to fear comparison with their opponents either in Church or State. It may be true that there were small men among them, men bitter and narrow and rude, but so there were among those on the other side; and when all abatements have been made, and all has been said that can be said in the way of caricature and depreciation, it still remains true that the sacred cause of liberty owes much to these men, and that the Puritan strain has entered into much that is best in our national life and literature.

But while there have been manifestations of the Puritan spirit in different ages and in varying form, there was a distinct and definite period in English history which has come to be recognized as that of Puritanism proper. This was a period of a hundred years, from the accession of Queen Elizabeth in 1558 to the death of Oliver Cromwell in 1658. Previous to the first of these dates the controversy was between Romanist and Protestant, during the century referred to it was waged between Anglican and Puritan, and we can trace Puritanism taking, as an historical movement, a definite line including its rise, development, ascendancy, and ultimate downfall.

The accession of Queen Elizabeth brought the English people to what we may call the parting of the ways. It was the introduction of a new era both for Church and State. Henry VIII came to the throne in 1509, and Elizabeth a few days before the beginning of 1559. During the half century between these two dates England was governed by three sovereigns of the House of Tudor and passed through three revolutions in her national Church life. At Henry's accession the Church in England was an organic portion of the Western Church, an extension into England of the one great Catholic Church of the West. Within this extension the Pope was supreme in all ecclesiastical causes; the highest Court of Appeal was at Rome; the highest officers of the Church were appointed by the

MARTIN BUCER

Pope; and as far back as the long reign of Henry III the Pope appointed Italian ecclesiastics not only to English bishoprics, but also to the ordinary livings of the Church. Then, in 1534, came the Reformation, and the Church *in* England became the Church *of* England. Various Acts of Parliament, but chiefly the great Act of Supremacy, transferred the papal authority to the King, and made Henry VIII, in everything but in name, Pope of England. It only remained for Pope Paul III to complete the process, which he did by issuing a Bull of Excommunication and deposition against the King and his abettors.

There was an important difference between the way the Reformation took its rise in England and the course it took among the protestant nations of the Continent. In Switzerland and Germany the movement began with the people; in England, on the contrary, it took its rise from the action of the State as a decisive movement and, for the most part, spread among the people afterwards. This accounts for the fact that when Edward VI came to the throne in 1547 the externals of worship were but little changed from their ancient form. The altars in the churches stood as of old; the priests wore their gorgeous vestments and celebrated their masses as before. And so long as this was the case and the Church service went on as it had done all their lives and those of their fathers before them, the people generally troubled their heads very little about changes in legislation. But Edward VI had not long been king before new ways came in. In the spring of 1548 a service-book in English instead of in Latin was prepared, and issued with authority the following year. The first English Book of Common Prayer took the place of the Mass, which in itself was a momentous fact; and stone altars gave place to communion tables. Still further, the leaders of the English Church entered into close and friendly relations with the ministers of the Reformed Churches of the Continent. So much so, indeed, that Peter Martyr and Martin Bucer came over at Cranmer's request to assist him in the preparation of the Articles and in the revision of the First Prayer Book of 1549, preparatory to the one of 1552.

It was a revolution again, which came in when in 1553 Queen Mary ascended the English throne. In her first proclamation of August 18 she expressed a wish that her people should be of the old religion, "the one she had ever professed from her infancy hitherto." One of the first Acts of her first Parliament was the Act of Repeal which abolished nine Acts passed in the reign of Edward VI, and restored the Church to the condition in which it was at the death of Henry VIII. Her second Act of Repeal, of 1554, abolished eighteen Acts of Henry relating to the Church, and one of Edward, thus restoring the Church to the condition in which it was in 1529 before the breach with Rome. England was again reconciled to the Papal See, and received absolution for her supposed sin of departure from the true faith. In meekness and docility she returned to the Roman obedience, and the power of the Catholic clergy became what it had been when the Pope constituted Henry VIII Defender of the Faith. But while restoring the ancient Church to its former ascendancy she did so in a spirit so ruthless that in the end it was found to have defeated itself. She outraged the better feeling of the nation by burning worthy men and women at the stake, so that while she overthrew the work of her father and her brother, hers also in turn came to be overthrown. It is but little indeed of the Acts and deeds of her government that took permanent place in the Constitution or laws of England. It has been truly said that her cruelties, her martyr-fires by "the loathing which they produced in the minds of Englishmen did more to establish the Reformation than any other single cause."

At the same time there were other causes at work as well. Even in the earlier days of Henry VIII the New Learning had begun to influence the minds of men and to change their attitude to the old ideas. In its conflict with old institutions and ancient modes of thought, it had with it as a mighty ally the newly-discovered power of the printing press. A new world was come to its birth time. It is said that most of the young men of brains and energy who grew to manhood during Mary's reign were lapsing from Catholicism and that educated women were falling faster and further.

There is one fact connected with the reign of Mary to which special attention must be called as being fundamental to the historical development of Puritanism. Many of the leading men who had embraced protestantism in the reigns of Henry and Edward found, as soon as the new Queen came to the throne, that England was no longer a place of safety for them. Burnet says that more than a thousand of these men sought refuge among the Reformed Churches of the Continent. Strype adds that among these exiles there were five bishops, five deans, four archdeacons, and fifty-seven doctors of divinity and preachers who had held these offices in the Church under Edward VI. It is to be noted that these men sought refuge not in the Lutheran cities of North Germany but among the Zwinglian and Calvinistic peoples of Switzerland and the Upper Rhine. This fact is thought to indicate that the English Church in the time of Edward VI was more Zwinglian than Lutheran, in its view of the sacraments than is sometimes supposed.

While the exiles found homes in various cities, in Frankfort, Strasburg, Bale, Zurich and Geneva, Zurich seems to have been their most important centre. Here during the five years of Mary's ill-starred reign they remained, forming friendships of closest Christian affection which have their record in the extensive body of letters preserved in the archives of the city, and which were written to Bullinger and other brethren after their return. But what is more to our purpose they were brought into close contact with the doctrines and discipline of the foreign reformers. They were favorably impressed with the simpler Church polity, to which they became accustomed, and were attracted to what seemed to them the more scriptural and spiritual forms of worship. The impressions thus received and the opinions they then came to hold had direct influence upon the course of events in the days near at hand.

Their time of return came at length when on the 17th of November, 1558, Mary passed away and Elizabeth was proclaimed queen in her stead. Sandys, who was then at Strasburg, heard the news on the 19th of December, and passed it on to the brethren at Zurich and Geneva. All prepared to return at once. The winter was, however, unusually severe, the roads in places almost impassable, and, the Rhine being frozen hard, sailing was impracticable. Those who started from Zurich were no less than fifty-seven days on the return journey. But rough and tedious as that journey was it was nevertheless cheered by a rising hope, the hope, as they expressed it, "that we may teach and practise the true knowledge of God's Word which we have learned in this our banishment, and by God's merciful providence seen in the best Reformed Churches." That is to say, these protestant exiles returned to England with foreign ideals in their minds which they hoped to be able to realize in the government and worship of the English Church at home.

Meantime Elizabeth had been already welcomed to the throne as the cherished hope of the protestant part of the nation. Young as she was she had seen strange sides of life and gone through rough experiences. Still, she had embraced the ideas of the later policy of her father, had entered into the spirit of the New Learning, and had expressed approval of a reform of the Church in accordance with a fuller understanding of Scripture and Christian antiquity. At the service held on Christmas Day, and therefore only a few days after her accession, she forbade the elevation of the Host, and on Bishop Oglethorpe, who was the celebrant, refusing to obey, she went out after the reading of the Gospel. Her feeling was still more marked on the more important occasion of the Coronation Service held on the 13th of January. Oglethorpe again officiated, again she commanded him to celebrate without the elevation, and again he refused. So she also took her own line of action, and just before the time when elevation would take place she retired to her "traverse" or dressing-room. On another state occasion, at the opening of Parliament, when she was met by the last abbot of Westminster with monks and candles, she unceremoniously bade him "Away with those torches; we can see well enough!"

Still, in spite of these manifestations the more advanced protestants could not feel quite sure of her.

She had told De Feria, the Spanish ambassador, that she acknowledged the Real Presence in the sacrament, and did now and then pray to the Virgin Mary. On another occasion also she explained to him that her religion was that of all sensible people who looked upon all the differences between the different versions of Christianity as little more than a mere bagatelle. The feeling of uncertainty concerning her thus created is reflected in the letters from England preserved in the archives of Zurich. One of the returned exiles, writing to a friend in that city, says: "If the Queen herself would but banish the Mass from her private chapel the whole thing might easily be got rid of." John Jewell, also, afterwards bishop of Salisbury, writes in much the same strain: "As to ceremonies and maskings there is a little too much foolery. That little silver cross of ill-omened origin still maintains its place in the Queen's Chapel." In a further letter to Peter Martyr he adds: "The scenic apparatus of divine worship is now under agitation: and those very things which you and I have so often laughed at are now seriously and solemnly entertained by *certain persons* as if the Christian religion could not exist without something tawdry. We cannot make these fooleries of much importance."

The first public act of Elizabeth, as it was with Mary, was to issue a proclamation forbidding any change being made in the forms of worship till Parliament met and settled the future order by statute. This first Parliament of

Elizabeth's reign met on the 25th of January, 1559, and sat till the 8th of May, to begin the "alterations of religion." After restoring to the Crown the first-fruits and tenths which Mary had returned to the Church, and repealing such penal laws as had been enacted against the service used under Edward VI, the Houses passed the two great memorable Acts of this Parliament, the Act of Supremacy and the Act of Uniformity, the two pillars on which the Church of England has rested down to our own day. The Act of Supremacy repealed Mary's Act of Repeal, and restored the ancient Jurisdictions and pre-eminencies appertaining to the Imperial Crown, but with one important change. Henry VIII and Edward VI had each claimed to be Supreme *Head* of the Church of England. Elizabeth was unwilling to be so described, maintaining as she did that this honor belongs to Christ and to Christ alone. She was therefore entitled Supreme *Governor*, the oath prescribed to be taken by all and every ecclesiastical person being to the effect that the Queen's Highness is the only supreme governor of this realm, as well in all spiritual or ecclesiastical things or causes as temporal, and that no foreign prince or prelate hath any ecclesiastical or spiritual authority within her dominions. Still while the Queen renounced the Headship of the Church the Act of the Submission of the Clergy was restored in full so that it was only the mere title that was renounced, and the whole power was reserved to the Crown. There was fierce battle round the Supremacy Bill for two whole months, from February 9 till April 29, but after renewed debates, changes and concessions it was finally passed. Any person refusing to take the oath prescribed under this Act was to forfeit and lose all and every ecclesiastical and spiritual promotion, benefit and office, and every temporal and lay promotion and office which he held at the time of refusal; his emoluments should ease as though he were actually dead.

There was one section of the Act of Supremacy (1 Eliz. cap. i, sec. 18) of profound significance for coming time. The Queen and her successors were to have power, by letters patent under the Great Seal to appoint commissioners to exercise under the Crown all manner of jurisdictions and to visit, reform, redress, correct and amend all errors, heresies, and schisms which might come within the scope of spiritual or ecclesiastical power. In other words, while the two great Acts referred to revolutionized the ecclesiastical constitution, this commission was to carry out the Queen's visitation and enforce her injunctions, and that too without authority from or reference to any clerical or ecclesiastical authority whatsoever, except that which pertained to the Crown itself. These commissions were renewed from time to time, deriving their authority direct from the Crown under the Great Seal and held responsible not to the Church in any sense, nor even to Parliament, but to the Privy Council. These commissions, whether temporary, as in the case of the first, which completed its task at the end of October, 1559, or permanent, as in the case of the Court of High Commission of 1583, became the recognized mode by which the supremacy of the sovereign, with the aid of the Privy Council, was brought to bear upon the government of the Church of England independently alike of Parliament or Convocation. In Tudor times the *personal* government of the Church by the sovereign was complete, and not less complete under Elizabeth than under Henry VIII, Edward VI, or Queen Mary.

The first Parliament of Elizabeth is memorable in our history not only for the Act of Supremacy but also for the Act of Uniformity by which it was accompanied. The reforming party in the Church were agreed as to doctrine but not as to discipline and ceremonies. This Act was intended to secure uniformity in both. But it was found then, as often since, that the men most resolute in enforcing uniformity are the men who create the most serious divisions. The first thing to secure was the basis or standard. Before the assembling of Parliament there was a private consultation held at the house of Sir Thomas Smith in Gannon Row to discuss which Prayer Book, that of 1552 or the one of 1549, should be submitted to Parliament for consideration and with what suggested changes. The Service Book of 1552 being agreed upon, certain changes were made therein, probably to meet the wishes of the Queen. In the Communion Service the old words of delivery were prefixed to the new; the rubric which denied the "real and essential presence" was left out; the clause in the Litany which prayed for deliverance from the Bishop of Rome and from all his detestable enormities was also omitted. A further change made at the instance of the Queen, a change most distasteful to the Puritans, was the introduction of what is now known as the Ornaments rubric, framed for the retention of the priestly vestments as they had been in 1548 before the issue of the First Prayer Book of 1549. This was a distinctly reactionary step in the view of the more advanced protestants, setting aside as it did the legislation of 1553 which prohibited the use of alb, vestment and cope in the prefatory rubric to the Order for Daily Prayer.

The Act of Uniformity, having thus reestablished the Second Prayer Book of 1552, with alterations and additions, as the recognized order of public worship, also made its use imperative under pressure of certain pains and penalties which were certainly not wanting in stringency. It provided that a minister using any other form of service, or any other manner of celebrating the Lord's Supper, should for the first offence lose a year's income and be imprisoned for six months; for a second offence he should suffer deprivation of benefice, and for a third imprisonment for life. So far as the laity were concerned, absence from public worship without lawful or reasonable excuse brought the offender under pain of the censure of the Church, and subjected him to a fine of twelve pence for the use of the poor of his parish.

Such were some of the provisions of the Act of Uniformity which came into force on the 24th of June, 1559, one day after the Act of Supremacy. The lines of legislation being thus laid down by Parliament, the Queen under the powers conferred by the Act of Supremacy appointed a body of commissioners to make a general visitation of the kingdom and see the laws carried out. These commissions were appointed in companies according to districts, each company consisting of several noblemen and gentlemen, a divine, a doctor of civil law and one or more lawyers. For their guidance and common action certain instructions were provided which are known as the Injunctions of Elizabeth. They were based on the previous injunctions issued by King Edward in 1547, and consisted of fifty-three Articles. They appear to have been drawn up by the revisers of the Prayer Book and were distinctly protestant in tone. Injunctions 2 and 18, for example, ordered the putting away of all the old paraphernalia associated with the ancient forms of worship, and also the abolition of all ecclesiastical processions. They were intended to regulate the lives of the clergy and the subjects of their preaching. All ecclesiastical persons having cure of souls were, to the uttermost of their wit, knowledge and learning, to declare manifest and open, at least four times every year, that all foreign power had been taken away and abolished, and that the Queen's power within her realms is the highest power under God; they were forbidden to set forth or extol the dignity of any images, relics or miracles; and on other subjects were to preach a sermon at least once a quarter. They were to "take away, utterly extinct and destroy all shrines, coverings of shrines, all tables, candlesticks, trindals, and rolls of wax, pictures, paintings and all other monuments of feigned miracles, pilgrimages, idolatry and superstition so that there remain no memory of the same." As in recent times mere children unlearned and unable to read matins or mass had been made priests, such as these were no more to be admitted to any cure or spiritual function. There should be "a modest and distinct song so used in all parts of the common prayers in the Church that the same may be as plainly understood as if it were read without singing." Still "for the comforting of such that delight in music," either at the beginning or the end of common prayer it may be permitted that "there may be sung a hymn or suchlike song to the praise of Almighty God in the best sort of melody and music that may be conveniently devised," but still so "that the sentence of the hymn may be understood and perceived." Under the sanction of these and suchlike laws, and guided by these Injunctions, the commissioners appointed set forth in the summer of 1559 to reform and reconstruct the religious life of England of their time.

CHAPTER II

VESTMENTS *and* CEREMONIES

The task assigned to the commissioners, of making an ecclesiastical visitation through the various counties, was proceeded with soon after Parliament was dissolved. Jewell, writing to Peter Martyr in the month of August, says: "I am on the point of setting out upon a long and troublesome commission for the establishment of religion through Beading, Abingdon, Gloucester, Bristol, Bath, Wells, Exeter, Cornwall, Dorset and Salisbury, a journey of about seven hundred miles, and occupying about four months." It was theirs to see the two principal Acts of the recent Parliament carried into practical effect. The Act of Supremacy as superseding the authority of the Pope by that of the Queen bore mainly, of course, upon the Roman Catholics in the nation who were opposed to the Reformation altogether. The Act of Uniformity was intended to regulate and bring to one standard the forms of worship of the more advanced protestants, whose one desire was to see the Reformation carried further still.

The Roman Catholic bishops, at Elizabeth's accession had been greatly reduced in numbers by death; those who remained, with the single exception of Kitchin of Llandaff, resolved to resign their positions and refuse the Oath of Supremacy rather than accept the Queen as governor of the Church. Their example was followed by an abbot and an abbess, four priors, twelve deans, fourteen archdeacons, sixty canons or prebendaries, and a hundred of the beneficed clergy, together with fifteen heads of Colleges in Oxford and Cambridge. The majority of the unbeneficed clergy took the oath and kept their places as they had done through all the changes of the three last reigns. It is calculated that there were then about 9400 clergy, of whom only 192 refused the oath. The vicar of Bray was the type of a class. Anthony Kitchin contrived to retain possession of the bishopric of Llandaff from 1545 to 1567, taking all the incongruous oaths required by Henry VIII, Edward VI, Mary and Elizabeth—Jewell, after telling Peter Martyr that Dr. Smith the Regius Professor of Divinity had now at last recanted for the fifth time, said to him—"Go now and deny transubstantiation if you can!"

The Act of Uniformity, affecting as it did the Roman Catholics as well as the Puritans, was in their case carried out somewhat rigorously. In the case of the Queen herself but little change was made in the ritual of her own private chapel. Being fond of pomp and magnificence in worship as in everything else, she would not part with the altar or crucifix; the choristers and priests still appeared in their copes; the altar was furnished with rich plate, had gilt candlesticks with lighted candles and a massive silver crucifix in the midst; on solemn festivals there was special music; and the ceremonies observed by the knights of the garter in their adoration towards the altar—ceremonies which had been abolished by King Edward and restored by Queen Mary—were now retained. So that the service in the Queen's own chapel, save that it was rendered in English instead of Latin, was as showy and splendid as in the days of the Roman ritual.

But whatever may have been Elizabeth's own private tastes in worship, there can be no doubt that in the latter half of 1559 the commissioners empowered by her made great changes in the London churches generally, and especially in the cathedral church of St. Paul. According to Strype they took effectual care to have all the instruments and utensils of idolatry demolished and destroyed, such as the roods with Mary and John and the images of tutelary saints. They commanded the prebendaries and arch-deacon to see that St. Paul's be stripped of all images and idols, and that in place of the altar a decent table should be provided for the celebration of the Lord's Supper. The people, too, with the memories of Smithfield fires strong within them, joined in the crusade. They attended upon the commissioners, carried into Cheapside, St. Paul's Churchyard and Smithfield, roods, crucifixes, the vestments of the priests, copes and surplices, banners and altar-cloths, books and Good Friday sepulchers; and all that could be burnt they burnt to ashes.

Turning now to the protestants and to the way in which the Act of Uniformity affected them, we find them already dividing themselves into two parties which we may describe as court reformers and Puritans. While there was difference between them on some points, on one point there was absolute agreement. They were both against toleration; both believed not only in uniformity but also in its enforcement by thsoue sword of the civil power. What they did differ about was as to what was the standard of uniformity, the one side upholding the Queen's supremacy and the law of the land, the other the Scriptures and the decrees of provincial and national synods. The court party and the majority of the bishops while admitting that the Scriptures were a perfect rule of faith, contended that they were not also an authoritative standard of discipline and church government, these matters being left by our Lord and His Apostles to the discretion of the civil magistrate. The Puritans, on the contrary, maintained that in discipline as well as in doctrine nothing should be imposed as necessary which could not be proved from Scripture. They held that what Christ has left indifferent man should not insist upon, for we are bidden to stand fast in the liberty wherewith Christ has made us free. They could not accept as indifferent, but rejected as unlawful, rites and ceremonies which, as experience showed, tended to idolatry and superstition. Christ, said they, is the sole lawgiver in His Church, and such things as are really necessary He Himself has enjoined to be observed to the end of the world. Their own experience of kingly interference in matters religious had not been without its lessons. They could not forget Henry's Act of Six Articles, the whip of six strings, as it was called; the dread memories of Mary's reign, too, were of painfully recent date and the Puritans felt themselves drawn to the forms of ecclesiastical polity prevailing among the Reformed Churches of Switzerland with whom they had so recently enjoyed Christian fellowship. Thus in Protestantism there was at this early stage a right and a left wing, not unlike the differences sometimes found in a modern political party.

While the new Injunctions had made great changes in the forms of worship, and that in a protestant direction, there was a provision in the 30th Article which caused great searchings of heart. This required that "all persons admitted into any vocation ecclesiastical, or into any society of learning in either of the Universities should use and wear such habits and garments and such square caps as were most commonly or orderly received in the last year of the reign of Edward VI." This was really a revival of what was called the Vestiarian Controversy, which had stirred great feeling ever since the day when Hooper on being made bishop of Gloucester refused to wear the vestments usually worn by bishops at their consecration. He called them the livery of Antichrist, and even obtained the King's permission to decline the bishopric on that account, only yielding at length to the earnest entreaty of other bishops and on the understanding that he might lay the vestments aside after wearing them at his consecration. To him and to men of his mind the garments used at mass were a significant symbol of ecclesiastical tendency as the flag of a nation is a significant symbol of cherished nationality. It was the outward and visible sign of a system which, in their souls, they had cast away from them. This controversy had never really altogether died out, as the letters sent to friends in Zurich remain to testify. Jewell, afterwards bishop of Salisbury, tells Peter Martyr that the doctrine of the Church is most pure, "but as to ceremonies and maskings there is a little too much foolery…God alone knows what will be the issue. The slow-paced horses retard the chariot." Sampson, afterwards dean of Christ Church, asks the same friend: "Should we not rather quit the ministry of the Word and Sacraments, than that these relics of the Amorites should be admitted?" Thomas Lever, master of St. John's College, Cambridge, in Edward's time, writes that the Injunctions "having prescribed to the clergy some ornaments such as the mass-priests formerly had and still retain, a great number of the clergy are now resuming similar habits, as they say, for the sake of obedience." And finally, Edwin Sandys, afterwards bishop of Worcester, wrote to Martyr in 1560 telling him, among other things, that "the popish vestments remain in our Church, I mean the Copes, which, however, we hope will not last long."

Such was the mental attitude of these men between Elizabeth's first Parliament in 1559 and her second Parliament which was opened on the 12th of January, 1563. What is of consequence, however, is that at the same time with this second Parliament there met also a Convocation which was destined to leave an enduring mark on the Church of England. It met at St. Paul's, and under letters of advice from the Queen calling for a review of the doctrine and discipline of the Church, proceeded first with the subject of doctrine. Archbishop Parker, somewhat elate with the idea that the time had arrived when the Church would be allowed to legislate for herself, opened the proceedings with the buoyant remark—"Behold the opportunity come for reforming the Church of England!" The first thing that was done was the carrying through of a revision of Cranmer's Articles of 1551, as a theological guide for the clergy in their public teaching. After being reduced to the number of thirty-nine at which they still remain, these Articles were sent to the Queen for the required authority under the Great Seal.

So far all was plain sailing, for on the matter of doctrine both sides were fairly agreed. But after this, Convocation proceeded to the discussion of the more thorny question of rites and ceremonies, and on reopening thus the whole ecclesiastical settlement on its ceremonial side, the relative strength of parties was plainly made manifest. To begin with, an overture was presented, bearing thirty-three signatures, including those of five deans, the provost of Eton, twelve archdeacons, and fourteen proctors or representatives, and demanding, among other things, that at the celebration of the Lord's Supper the posture of kneeling, as suggesting the adoration of the elements, should be left indifferent; that the sign of the cross in baptism should be disused; that the wearing of copes and surplices be abolished, so that all ministers should use "a grave and comely side garment" or preaching gown; and that they should not be compelled to wear such caps and gowns as the Romish clergy.

This overture not being approved, a motion was then brought forward to the effect that while Sundays and the special feasts associated with the events of our Savior's life should be religiously observed, all other holidays should be abolished; that in all parish churches the minister in common prayer should turn his face to the people; that the cross in baptism be omitted; that kneeling at the sacrament be left to the discretion of the minister; and that it should suffice if he wear the surplice once, provided that no minister should say service or minister the sacraments but in comely garment or habit. After some discussion this motion was carried to the vote, when it appeared there was a majority in its favor by forty-three against thirty-five. But the proxies had then to be counted and these reversed the decision by one vote and only one, there being now fifty-eight for the motion and fifty-nine against. So that by the vote of one man, who was not present at the debate—that "odd, shy man"—as he has been called, it was thus determined to make no alteration in the ceremonies, and the Court party, therefore, carried their point in that memorable Convocation.

It remained now to be seen what effect this decision would have upon the country at large. There being a visitation of the plague in 1563, there was not much done that year in the way of enforcing uniformity in the matter of the vestments. Many of the parochial clergy had an aversion to the prescribed habits; sometimes they wore them, but more frequently they did not. Occasionally a refractory minister would be cited before the spiritual courts and there admonished, and so the matter ended. But at length more peremptory steps were taken. A document bearing date February 14, 1564, was laid before the Queen setting forth the irregularities prevailing in the order of Church service. She was greatly incensed by this report, and especially that so little heed was paid to her laws, for she regarded the Church as hers and held that in all matters pertaining to it her will should be paramount. She therefore addressed a letter to the two archbishops directing them to inquire as to what diversities in doctrine, rites and ceremonies prevailed among the clergy, and to take effectual methods for securing an exact order and uniformity.

The Puritans tried to avert the storm they saw to be approaching. One of their most trusted leaders, Dr. Pilkington, the bishop of Durham, laid their case before the Earl of Leicester, seeking his interest with the Queen on their behalf. He pleaded that compulsion should not be used in things of liberty, and urged his lordship to consider how all protestant countries had cast away popish apparel along with the Pope, while England was resolving to keep to it as a holy relic. He was sure, he said, that many ministers would rather lose their livings than comply, and that, too, at a time when there was great scarcity of teachers, many places having none at all. But all pleas were alike unavailing. The Queen gave command to Archbishop Parker to proceed at once in the enforcement of uniformity, a command he obeyed with vigor and resolution. So much excitement prevailed that Bishop Jewell in a sermon preached at St. Paul's Cross endeavored to throw oil on the troubled waters. He said he was not there to defend the prescribed habits; his purpose was rather to show that the things prescribed were, after all, only matters of indifference. Still they were insisted upon. Under the title of "Advertisements" Archbishop Parker issued certain Articles apparently without the royal sanction or authority. They were described as "certain orders or rules thought meet and convenient though not prescribed as laws equivalent with the eternal Word of God, or as of necessity binding the conscience, but as temporal orders, mere ecclesiastical."

But though thus mildly described the Advertisements were sufficiently imperative. All licenses for preaching bearing date before March 1, 1564 were to be regarded as void and of none effect, but would be renewed to those meet for office. In the matter of the vestments it was ordered that in cathedrals and collegiate churches the officiating minister at the Communion should use a cope; that deans and prebends should wear a surplice with a silk hood, in the choir; every minister saying public prayer or administering sacraments should wear a comely surplice with sleeves, to be provided at the charges of the parish. In their common apparel abroad all deans of cathedral churches, masters of colleges, archdeacons and other dignitaries having any ecclesiastical living were to wear side gowns with sleeves straight at the band without any tailing cape, and to wear tippets of sarcenet.

To some of the bishops the enforcing of the Advertisements proved a very unwelcome task. Bishop Jewell writing to his friend Bullinger in 1566, says: "The contest about the surplice is not yet at rest. I wish that all, even the slightest vestige of popery might be removed from our churches, and above all from our minds. But the Queen at this time is unable to endure the least alteration in the matter of religion." The nonconforming Puritans felt they were entitled to claim that the bishops in enforcing the orders upon their clergy were doing so only under constraint and not by conviction. They were temporizing, but for themselves they could not temporize. They could not look upon these vestments as matters of indifference, associated as they had been with Romanism and the evil days of Mary's reign. In July, 1566, Humphrey and Sampson writing to Bullinger asked: "How can that habit be thought to be consistent with the simple ministry of Christ which used to set off the theatrical pomp of the Romish priesthood? Our opponents are the real innovators. In Bang Edward's time the Lord's Supper was celebrated in simplicity in many places without the surplice. The cope was then abrogated by law and is now being restored after abrogation. This is not to extirpate popery but to replant it; not to advance in religion but to go backward. Why should we borrow anything from popery? Why should we not agree in rites as well as in doctrine with the other Reformed Churches? It is only seven years ago that we regained our liberty, why should we go back to servitude? There is danger in these practices; they are insidious; they do not shew themselves all at once, but creep on little by little. Why cannot the bishops endure us who formerly bore the same cross with them and who now preach the same Christ? Why do they cast us into prison? Why do they persecute us on account of the habits? Why do they spoil us of our substance and means of subsistence?" In this urgent manner the president of Magdalen College and the dean of Christ Church put the case on behalf of themselves and their Puritan brethren. Turner, dean of Bath and Wells, a man of versatile learning and still remembered as one of the early founders of science, when preaching in his cathedral asked, with a feeling of indignation: "Who gave the bishops more authority over me than I over them, either to forbid me or to deprive me, unless they have it from their holy father the Pope?"

The nonconforming clergy claimed that they had an equal right with the conformist to say the Church of England was theirs. Indeed they were not without hope that the future of that Church would be with them. They remembered that when the decision in Convocation went against them in 1563, it did so by only one vote, and that a proxy vote; so that there at least parties proved to be of nearly even strength. And there were not wanting signs that in the community at large they were increasing in strength and influence. Among the laity there were not a few who were quite as averse to the habits as they were themselves. With increasing dislike to popery there was increasing dislike to the vestments, many refusing to go to the churches where they were worn. Even Whitgift recorded that the clergy who did wear them were sometimes rudely assailed in the streets as time-servers and papists in disguise. There were some people at least who could not forget that only ten years ago friends and neighbors of theirs had been burnt at the stake in Mary's time. To them therefore the vestments seemed almost as if they were stained with the blood of the martyrs. And not merely among the common people, the Puritans had reason to know, there was sympathy with them, but also in high places, even in the Court itself, with men like Secretary Cecil, the Earl of Leicester, Sir Francis Knollys and the Earls of Bedford and Warwick. Meantime the archbishop persisted in his policy of coercion. Among those whom he cited to Lambeth were Sampson and Humphrey with whom he entered into conference on the points at issue. They afterwards appealed to him by letter pleading that conscience is a very tender thing and all men cannot look upon the same things as being indifferent.

They also made their appeal to antiquity, to the practice of the other Reformed Churches in their own day and even to the consciences of the bishops themselves. It so happened that at the very time these conferences were going forward, Sampson and Humphrey were both selected as the preachers at St. Paul's Cross during Lent, an appointment regarded as a mark of distinction. The archbishop was indignant, and writing to Cecil he said: "This appointment is not by me; by whom I know not: either by the Bishop of London or the Lord Mayor." Being thus incensed he had the two men before him again and peremptorily commanded them either to conform or to leave their posts. They merely replied that their consciences would not permit them to comply with his injunctions, come what might. Upon this they were then and there committed to prison; and as Sampson's deanery was in the gift of the Crown he was deprived of his office at once. The same experience came to Humphrey somewhat later on. When he also was deprived, he sent an earnest remonstrance to the commissioners in which he says: "Since the mass attires be so straitly commanded, the mass itself may shortly be looked for. A sword is now put into the hands of those that under Queen Mary have drawn it for popery. The painful preacher for his labour is beaten, the unpreaching prelate offending in greater escapeth scot-free. The learned man without his cap is afflicted, the capped man without learning is not

MARY TUDOR

touched. Is not this directly to break the laws of God? Is not this to prefer man's will before faith, judgement and mercy, man's traditions before the ordinances of God? We confess one faith of Jesus Christ, we preach one doctrine, we acknowledge one ruler in earth over all things. Shall we be used so for a surplice? Shall brethren persecute brethren for a forked cap devised of singularity of him that is our foreign enemy? Oh that ever I saw this day, that ever our adversaries should laugh to see brethren fall together by the ears!"

The cases of Sampson and Humphrey, leading Oxford men, came to a final issue towards the end of April, 1565. Then about the middle of October of that same year the state of things in the sister University of Cambridge came under review. There the movement in favor of the Protestant Reformation took shape early. As far back as 1510 Erasmus, after being at Louvain and Oxford, came to Cambridge in search of a new field of labor, taking up his residence, under Fisher's protection, in Queens' College. Between 1511 and 1515 he there wrote his *Novum Instrumentum* which did much to prepare the way for protestantism, and the light he kindled was kept burning. Later on a little band of Cambridge scholars met together by stealth for the discussion of Martin Luther's earlier treatises, William Tyndale, the ever-memorable translator of the English Bible, who was resident in the University from 1514 to 1521, being one of them. A recent historian of

the University records that while it was the taunt of their
adversaries that the members of this brotherhood were
mostly young men, it is certain that they were among
the most able and diligent of the student class of the
time, and their influence made numerous converts. He
goes on to say that the best scholarship of the University
was represented among them, as is proved by the fact
that when Cardinal Wolsey was founding his college
at Oxford, and was for that purpose selecting from
Cambridge the most efficient teachers and lecturers, no
fewer than six out of the eight thus chosen were notable
supporters of the Reformation doctrine. The leaven had
thus been working for more than a generation when in
the autumn of 1565 the prevalence of Puritanism came
to be matter for serious inquiry. It arose, first of all, as
affecting certain licenses to preach. Pope Alexander VI,
during his occupancy of the See of Rome (1492-1503)
granted to the University of Cambridge the privilege of
licensing twelve ministers yearly, to preach anywhere
throughout England without obtaining license from any
of the bishops. These were licensed under the common
seal of the University, and this privilege was renewed in
the letters patent granted by Queen Elizabeth, and was
retained and made use of to further the more advanced
forms of Reformation. George Withers, one of the
preachers thus licensed, went so far in his protestant
zeal as to break certain "superstitious" painted windows

in the college chapels on which the use of prayers for the dead was enjoined. Upon this he was summoned to appear before the archbishop at Lambeth where he "refused to enter bonds for wearing of the cornered cap." This led to further inquiry which proved conclusively that nonconformity in the matter of the vestments was more widely spread in the University than had been supposed. Proceedings were therefore taken at once, and, in expectation of a proclamation of enforcement, a petition was forwarded to Cecil, at that time chancellor of the University, praying him to use his influence with the Queen that they might not be compelled to revive a popish habit which they had laid aside. They took leave to assure him, as in the presence of God, that nothing but reason and the quiet enjoyment of their consciences had led them to take the course they had taken. Many in the University of piety and learning, they said, were convinced of the unlawfulness of the habits, therefore, if conformity should be insisted upon, they would be compelled to resign their positions, and so, by rigor and imposition both religion and learning would suffer. The first of the signatures to this petition was that of the vice-chancellor, Dr. Beaumont, master of Trinity, who had himself been one of the exiles in Zurich in Mary's time. Other signatures were those of Kelk, master of Magdalene, Button, master of Pembroke, and Longworth, master of St. John's. Curious to relate there was also attached to this petition the signature of John Whitgift, fellow of Peterhouse and Lady Margaret professor, who in after years, as archbishop of Canterbury, was to be the resolute persecutor of the Puritans. This petition was ill-taken by the chancellor who wrote to the vice-chancellor requiring him to call together the heads of colleges and let them know that if they valued Christianity, the honor of the University, and the favor of the Queen they must continue the use of the habits.

It was at St. John's college that discontent first showed itself in violent outbreak. A young man named Fulke had "lefte of wearing a square cappe and used a hatte," and both at St. Mary's and in the college chapel had preached in strong terms against the use of the surplice. Upon this the college was roused to a high pitch of excitement, and "in fine they waxed so hot that they could abide no such garment upon them." The climax was reached at a festival in October when Longworth, the master, was—it is suggested, intentionally—absent from college. On Saturday evening, October 12, at the first tolling of the bell for prayers a number of the youths of the house rushed into the chapel without surplices, and more than that, hissed at those who came after with their surplices on. The master on his return on hearing of what had taken place practically ranged himself and the University on the side of the malcontents. The other side sent in a set of articles accusatory and urged the chancellor to take action, but Cecil was slow and Longworth seemed quite indifferent, saying that he knew the real mind of the chancellor more than most people. However, he and several of the refractory students were sent for to London, but it came to the ears of people in Cambridge that the master had been very favorably entertained both by Cecil and the bishop of London. In the end Cecil drew up an easy form of retraction which Longworth signed with the promise that it should be read before the college on his return. But as the outbreak spread to other colleges, and especially to Trinity, Cecil took up the matter more seriously. He then wrote to the vice-chancellor describing this nonconformity as "a wilful breaking of common order, a lewd leprosy of libertines," and requiring him to call together the heads of houses, urging them to unity, and further recommending that preachers who had opposed the use of the vestments should be inhibited for a time from preaching and lecturing. "Nevertheless," says Neal, "the University of Cambridge was still a sanctuary for Puritans."

The colleges having been thus dealt with, the archbishop began to devise means by which he could make London less Puritanical. Grindal was at that time bishop of this important diocese, and though he had himself been one of the Zurich exiles, and was in sympathy with simpler ways of worship, yet irregularities prevailing, and the Queen's anger thereat, led him to join the archbishop in his crusade on behalf of uniformity.

At this point, Beaumont, the master of Trinity, put the direct question to Cecil whether, under the Act, he had power to deprive a man merely because he declined to wear a surplice, seeing that penalty had not been attached to disobedience in the Queen's Injunctions. This point the archbishop also was debating in his mind and was not clear upon it. He sought legal advice on this matter of deprivation, but got little guidance: "I must say this much more that some lawyers be in opinion that it is hard to proceed in deprivation having no more warrant but the Queen's Majesty's word of mouth." However, after being much tossed to and fro in his mind and consulting with his brother bishops he determined to run the risk. He would call before himself and the bishop of London all pastors and curates of the city, would try to win them to conformity by setting forth the penalty of disobedience; would then examine them one by one, and obtain, if possible, a promise of conformity in ministration, testified by subscription of their hands; then to suspend all who should refuse. He felt he was taking a strong course of action and was not without misgiving. By way of strengthening his own wavering resolution he sought the countenance of eminent laymen to stand by him. "We trust," he wrote to Cecil, "that the Queen's Majesty will send some honourable to join with us two, to authorise her commandment and pleasure." The day before the eventful meeting he wrote again hoping for the presence of Cecil himself, also for that of the Lord Keeper Bacon and the Marquess of Northampton, inviting them to dine with him, and asking to be certified of their coming. But they would have none of it. They agreed that it was the archbishop's work, not theirs, and they resolved to leave him to it.

Tuesday, March 26, 1566, was the fateful date on which the clergy of London were cited to appear before Parker and the bishop of London at Lambeth. As he could prevail upon no layman, or any of the nobility, or members of council to join him, he obtained the presence of the dean of Westminster and a few canonists for the occasion. In response to his summons about a hundred and ten ministers presented themselves, nine or ten being absent. To secure that the demand he was about to make should be quite clear and definite there was provided for their inspection a clergyman properly dressed according to the pattern prescribed by the regulations. Robert Cole, the rector of St. Mary le Bow, a non-conforming minister who had been brought to compliance, consented to stand there to show how the Queen wished them to be attired when discharging their ecclesiastical functions. It is difficult to restrain a smile at the narrative, for it reads like a passage of mordant satire from *Sartor Resartus*. After some preliminary efforts at persuasion the chancellor of the London diocese became the spokesman of the occasion. "My masters and the ministers of London," said he, "the Council's pleasure is that strictly ye keep the unity of apparel like to this man, as ye see him: that is, a square cap, a scholar's gown priestlike, or tippet, and in the Church a linen surplice: and inviolably observe the rubric of the Book of Common Prayer, and the Queen's Majesty's Injunctions and the Book of Convocation. Ye that will presently subscribe, write *Volo*. Those that will not subscribe, write *Nolo*. Be brief: make no words." Some of them attempted to speak, "Peace, peace," said the chancellor. "Apparitor, call the churches. Masters answer presently *sub poena contemptus*: and set your names." The apparitor, or summoner, called the names of the churches; first of the peculiars of Canterbury; then of the incumbents of Southwark in Winchester diocese; then of the London clergy. Parker writing to Cecil the same day told him that thirty-seven refused to conform—"of which number were the best and some preachers." The rest submitted. Of those who refused he says: "In fine we did suspend them and sequester their fruits and from all manner of ministry. They showed reasonable quietness and modesty, otherwise than I looked for. I think some of them will come in when they shall feel their want." So Archbishop Parker coldly thought, unconsciously measuring himself while measuring them. There he was wrong. They were resolute Englishmen, had counted the cost and had no thought for a moment of returning on their steps. Not that they did not feel the consequences keenly: "We are killed in our souls," said they, "for that we cannot perform in the singleness of our hearts this our ministry." It was this and not the mere pinch of possible bodily want that touched them. Still all must be faced. "We have thought good," they further say, "to yield ourselves into the hands of men, to suffer whatsoever God hath appointed us to suffer for the preferring of the commandments of God and a clear conscience before the commandments of men .... Not despising men, therefore, but trusting in God only, we seek to serve Him with a clear conscience so long as we shall live here, assuring ourselves that those things we shall suffer for doing so shall be a testimony to the world, that great reward is laid up for us in heaven, where we doubt not but to rest for ever with them that have before our days suffered for the like."

CHAPTER III

The PURITANS *and the* HIERARCHY

The separation made at Lambeth palace between the consenting and non-consenting clergy had more significance and farther-reaching consequences than could be realized at the time. The decided action then taken by the authorities of the Church led to yet more resolute advance on the part of the dissentients, so that the question soon came to be one, not merely of vestments and forms of ritual, but of the whole hierarchical system on which the Church was based. A dividing line, with parties ranged on separate sides, may be traced from that day down to our own times.

Of the clergy deprived on March 26, 1566, some betook themselves to the study and practice of medicine, others became chaplains in the families of the Puritan nobility and gentry; some went north and joined the presbyterian Church of Scotland while others emigrated to the Low Countries. It is to be feared that not a few were, with their families, reduced to sore straits of poverty. Of the remainder, not thus accounted for, five went the length of defying the interdict placed upon them, going to their churches and preaching as aforetime. For this act of disobedience they were summoned before the Queen in Council. They were given eight days wherein to visit their friends, after which they were committed as prisoners to the private custody of certain bishops, two being sent to the bishop of Winchester, two to the bishop of Ely, and one to the bishop of Norwich.

The withdrawal of so many London ministers from their parishes naturally led to considerable embarrassment in the conduct of services. Some churches had to be closed, there being no one to officiate. To one church on Palm Sunday six hundred persons came to receive the Communion, only to find the doors shut against them. The deprived ministers on their part issued a joint manifesto explanatory of the step they had felt compelled to take. Among other things they pointed out that neither the prophets of the Old Testament nor the apostles of the New were distinguished by their garments; that the linen vestment was the mark of that priesthood of Aaron which had been superseded by Christ and His Church. Historically speaking, they maintained that the distinction of garments in the Christian Church came in when antichrist came in; for the clergy of Ravenna, writing to the emperor in 876 A.D. said to him: "We are distinguished from the laity not by our clothes but by our doctrines, not by our habits but by our conversation." It was quite clear, they said, that the vestments in question had led to idolatry, had been an offence to weak Christians and an encouragement to the Romanists in the nation; and they contended that supposing these garments were indifferent, which they did not admit, that was a reason why they should not be made obligatory, this being an infringement of the liberty wherewith Christ had made them free. To this manifesto a printed reply was issued from the other side commending the attention of the seceders to those words of the apostle: "Let every soul be subject to the higher power."

After waiting for about eight weeks, to see if there might be any relenting on the part of the Queen and the archbishop, the ministers, and those of the Puritan party in the city who were in agreement with them, held solemn conference together, in which after prayer and serious debate as to the lawfulness and necessity of separation from the Established Church, they came to the following agreement: "That since they could not have the Word of God preached, nor the Sacraments administered without idolatrous gear; and since there had been a separate congergation in London, and another in Geneva in Mary's time, using a book and order of Service approved by Calvin, which was free from the superstitions of the English Service: therefore it was their duty, in their present circumstances, to break off from the public churches, and to assemble, as they had opportunity, in private houses or elsewhere to worship God in a manner that might not offend against the light of their consciences." Commenting on the serious step thus taken, Strype, the English Church historian, writes thus: "Here was the era or date of Separation: a most unhappy event whereby people of the same country, of the same religion, and of the same judgement in doctrine, parted communions; one part being obliged to go aside into secret houses and chambers, to serve God by themselves, which begat strangeness between neighbours, Christians and Protestants."

It soon became known that there were gatherings for worship in woods and private buildings, without the habits and ceremonies of the Church, whereupon the Queen sent an urgent message to the commission to take effectual steps to prevent the people leaving their parish churches, and to be careful to warn them of the consequences of frequenting separate conventicles. All the same the gatherings continued on through the winter till the following summer, when, on the 19th of June, 1567, a congregation of about a hundred people being met in Plumber's Hall for sermon and communion, the sheriffs of the city broke in upon them, taking many into custody. The next day several of these were called to appear before Grindal, bishop of London, and the lord mayor. The bishop reminded them that by these proceedings of theirs they were in effect condemning the Reformed Church of England, and those martyrs who had shed their blood for it. To this one of them replied that they condemned not others, but felt that for themselves they must stand to God's Word. Another—"the ancientest of them," added: "So long as we might have the Word freely preached and the sacraments administered without the preferring of idolatrous gear about it, we never assembled together in houses. But when it came to this that all our preachers were displaced by your law, so that we could hear none of them in any church by the space of seven or eight weeks, and were troubled and commanded by your Courts from day to day for not coming to our parish churches, then we bethought us what were best to do. And now if from the Word of God you can prove we are wrong we will yield to you and do open penance at Paul's Cross: if not we will stand to it by the grace of God." Eventually twenty-four men and seven women were committed to Bridewell prison for a twelvemonth and then released.

At this point the scene shifts from London to

Cambridge and the University becomes the centre of interest in the fortunes of Puritanism. New subjects begin to be debated and new leaders come to the front. Of these leaders the foremost was Thomas Cartwright, a fellow of Trinity, who is described as a man of genius and one who would have been prominent in any age. Thomas Fuller spoke of his fame as that of "a pure Latinist, accurate Grecian, exact Hebraist," and Theodore Beza was of opinion that he was the most learned man he knew. In 1562, when he became a fellow, he was already known in the University as an eloquent preacher and a rising theological scholar. On the occasion of Queen Elizabeth's visit to Cambridge in 1564 he was elected to take part in the theological disputation held in her presence, and stories have come down to us of the enthusiasm he created as University preacher, the windows of St. Mary's, it is said, having to be taken out that those might hear without who could not find entrance within. But what we are now more immediately concerned with is the fact that when towards the end of 1569 Dr. Chaderton resigned the Lady Margaret chair and became Regius Professor of Theology, Cartwright, at the age of thirty-four, became his successor. In the fulfillment of his office as Lady Margaret professor he gave a series of lectures on the early chapters of the Acts of the Apostles, in the course of which he assailed the hierarchical constitution of the Church. The position he took was that nothing should be established in the Church but what was enjoined in Scripture; that therefore the names and functions of archbishop and archdeacon should be abolished, and that the lawful ministers of the Church, bishops and deacons, should be reduced to the apostolic institution—the bishops to preach the Word of God and pray, while the deacons had the care of the poor. He held further that every church ought to be governed by its own minister and presbyters, not by the bishop's chancellor or the official of the archdeacon; and that bishops should not be created by the civil authority, but be freely chosen by the Church. On other points also he contended that no man ought to be admitted to the ministry unless he was able to preach; that as equal reverence was due to every part of Scripture and to all the revealed names of God, there is no reason why the people should stand at the reading of the gospel, or bow at the name of Jesus; that at the Communion it was as lawful to sit as to kneel or stand; that the sign of the cross in baptism is superstitious; that it is papistical to forbid marriages at certain times of the year; and that the observation of Lent and fasting on Friday is superstitious.

These, of course, were startling opinions to be uttered from a professor's chair, or worse, from the University pulpit, and Dr. Whitgift, then master of Trinity, entered into the lists against Cartwright. He also reported his proceedings to Sir William Cecil, the chancellor, and

QUEEN ELIZABETH I

eventually in combination with the vice-chancellor and other heads of the University, he obtained a body of new statutes giving larger powers. This was in the month of August, 1570. That same month Cartwright also wrote to Cecil, assuring him that he was contending for a discipline which not only in England but also in foreign nations was accompanied by the daily prayers of pious men; that what some men called novelties were really most ancient, and began with the Churches of Christ and His Apostles. Cecil, never an extreme churchman, urged on behalf of Cartwright that he spoke as he did, not from arrogance or ill-will, but as reader of the Scriptures had merely given notes by way of comparison between the orders of the ministry in the Apostles' time and those of the present Church of England. Whitgift and his party, however, were unwilling to take so lenient a view, and under the increased powers of the new statutes, Cartwright was first deprived of his professorship and fellowship and afterwards expelled from the University. In 1573 he went abroad and became minister of the Congregation of English Merchants at Antwerp and subsequently at Middelburg in Zealand.

The third Parliament of Elizabeth, summoned in 1571, sat from April 2 to May 29, when ecclesiastical matters were much in debate, and in the House of Commons there was a resolute and active party in sympathy with the Puritans. As their spokesman, Mr. Strickland, "an ancient gentleman," brought in a Bill on the 6th of April for the further reformation of the Church. As in a second speech, a week later, he was enforcing the provisions of this Bill, the treasurer of the Queen's household rose and reminded him that all matters of ceremonies were to be referred to the Queen, and that for the House to meddle with the royal prerogative was not convenient. Afterwards also the Queen herself, to show her displeasure at Strickland's motion, summoned him before her presence in Council and forbade him the Parliament House. This unconstitutional invasion of the liberties of the Commons led, however, to so many protesting speeches that the Queen, having the Tudor instinct of knowing when to retreat from an untenable position, recalled the prohibition on the 20th of April. On his return to the House Strickland proceeded further and moved that a Confession of Faith be published with the authority of Parliament, as in other protestant countries. This was assented to, and a committee was appointed which drew up certain Articles, which were really those of the Convocation of 1562, with, however, certain omissions. The archbishop asked why they had left out that for the consecration of bishops and others relating to the hierarchy; Peter Wentworth replied they had done so because they had not yet made up their minds as to whether they were agreeable to the Word of God or not. "But surely," said the archbishop, "in these things you will refer yourselves wholly to us, the bishops." With some warmth Wentworth replied that "they meant to pass nothing they did not understand; for that would be to make the bishops into popes: make you popes who list, for we will make you none." On the 1st of May a message was received from the Queen concerning this confirmation of the Articles of 1562: "The Queen's Majesty... mindeth to publish these and have them executed by the bishops, by direction of her Highness' Regal Authority of Supremacy of the Church of England; and not to have them dealt in by Parliament." Unmoved by this rebuke, the Commons, two days later, sent up to the Lords a "Bill for the ministers of the Church to be of sound religion." This when passed became the important Act of 13 Eliz. cap. xii., under which subscription to the Articles was first required. Before Christmas next following, every minister under the degree of a bishop was "to declare his assent and subscribe to all the Articles of Religion which only concern the confession of the true Christian faith and the doctrine of the sacraments comprised in the book of 1562, and bring from the bishop, in writing, under his seal authentic, proof of such assent and subscription." If he did not comply within the given time, he "shall be *ipso facto* deprived, and all his ecclesiastical promotions shall be void, as if he then were naturally dead."

In addition to the demand for subscription to the

Articles, which was a new thing, the Commissioners Ecclesiastical, when the parliamentary session was over, issued an order on the 7th of June to all churchwardens to the effect that they were in no wise to suffer any minister to minister any sacrament or say public prayers other than according to the Book of Common Prayer, and not thus unless his license to preach is dated after the 1st of May last. In the convocation of this year a Book of Canons was made, one of the requirements of which was that every bishop should, before September next, call before him all the clergy of his diocese, and require of them their faculties for preaching under authentic seal, only giving back these licenses to such ministers as he approved. Before, however, any licenses could be restored the ecclesiastical vestments were to be enforced. Upon refusal a minister was to resign quietly or be deprived. In pursuance of these orders the archbishop, early in June, cited some of the leading Puritans to Lambeth, Lever, Sampson, Goodman, Walker and Wiborne being among them; the same month Robert Browne, at that time chaplain to the Duke of Norfolk, and sometimes spoken of since as the founder of the Brownists, was also cited. In the northern province Whittingham and Gilby came under observation. Details of what happened in all cases have not come down to us, but it is said that through the action of the commissioners at this time about one hundred ministers suffered deprivation. Browne,

Harrison, and others went beyond sea to Zealand; and there is a curious document among the State Papers of this period (1566-1573) containing a proposal for transplanting the precisians, to the number of 3000 men, to Ireland, assigning them a portion of Ulster, "there, as concerning religion, to live according to the reformation of the best churches."

Parliament met again on the 8th of May, 1572, the lord keeper making the opening speech, in which, in the Queen's name, he recommended the Houses to see the laws relating to the Church carried into effect and to enact other laws, if needful, for that purpose. Instead, however, of making new laws for the enforcement of ceremonies, two Bills were introduced for their regulation, in one of which it was proposed to redress certain grievances complained of by the Puritans. Both these Bills passed the Commons and were referred to a select committee of both Houses. The Queen again resented this interference, as she regarded it, and through the speaker informed the Commons that it was her pleasure that no Bills on religion should be received without previous consent from the bishops, and she commanded that the two Bills concerning rites and ceremonies should be delivered up. Peter Wentworth again protested against this infringement of the liberty and free speech of Parliament. "Her Majesty," he said, "has forbidden us to deal with any matter of religion till we first receive it from the bishops. Then there is little hope of reformation. I have heard an old Parliament man say that the banishment of the pope, and the reforming of the true religion had its beginning from this House, not from the bishops." For this outspoken utterance of his Wentworth was sent to the Tower.

It was at this time the Puritans entered upon a new and important departure in their line of policy. Having lost all hope of effecting such reformation as they desired by appealing to the Queen or the bishops, they resolved to make their appeal to Parliament itself. At a meeting of the leaders held in London it was resolved to draw up a manifesto, which is now known as the First Admonition to Parliament. It was published anonymously in 1572, but was admitted to be the work of John Field, the minister of Alderbury, in conjunction with Thomas Wilcocks; and Strype records that it was so eagerly read that it went through four editions before the end of 1573. This manifesto is historically important as being a clear and deliberate declaration of what the Puritans had in view at this stage in the development: of their scheme of reformation. The Admonition began by asserting in the preface that till there was a right ministry of God and a right government of His Church there could be no right religion. They, therefore, present for the godly consideration of Parliament a true platform of a Church reformed. It would be seen that radical changes were needed, for as yet "we are scarce come to the outward face of the same. Those who were priests under Henry VIII and Mary ought to be removed, for they are still the Romanists at heart they always were. Then, when better men are sought, there ought to be an election of the minister by the elders with the common consent of the whole church. He should be *called* by the congregation, not thrust upon them by the bishop, or ordained without a title, and should be admitted to his function by the laying on of the hands of the eldership only. The officers of a church are chiefly three—ministers or pastors, elders and deacons. As for the elders not only their office but their very name has been removed out of the English Church, and in their stead we yet maintain the lordship of one man over many churches, yea over sundry shires. If you would restore the Church to her ancient officers this you must do: Instead of an archbishop or lord bishop you must make equality of ministers; instead of chancellors, archdeacons, officials, commissaries, proctors, summoners, church wardens and such like you have to plant a lawful and godly eldership. To these three jointly—ministers, elders and deacons—is the whole government of the Church to be committed. Amend therefore these abuses and reform God's Church and the Lord is on your right hand: let these things alone, and God who is a righteous judge will one day call you to your reckoning. Is a reformation good for France and can it be evil for England? Is discipline meet for Scotland and is it unprofitable for this realm? The right government of the Church cannot be separated from the doctrine of the Church."

The writers were conscious that the work Parliament was thus called upon to undertake was no light task:— "Your wisdoms have to remove advowsons, patronages, impropriations and bishops' authority and to bring in the old and true election which was accustomed to be made by the congregation. Remove homilies, articles, injunctions, and that prescript order of service made out of the Mass book; take away the lordship, the loitering, the pomp, the idleness and livings of bishops, but yet employ them to such ends as they were in the old Church appointed for."

Such in brief was the drift of the First Admonition, which produced a great sensation on its appearance in print. Its authors were at once committed to Newgate, and several of the bishops assailed the book as foolish as well as dangerous, to which a writer of the time replied that "foolish it may be, but it is still unanswered, and though there are scarce as many leaves in it as there are months past since it came forth, it is fleeing as a fire-brand from place to place and setting all the country on fire." At length it was decided to send forth an answer, which at the request of the primate was undertaken by Dr. Whitgift with the assistance of two of the bishops.

This work has been described as "a learned answer," and an "excellent book, containing a very satisfactory vindication of the Church, of England." Its two main positions are that we are not bound of necessity to keep to the same form of church government as obtained in the time of the Apostles and that it is unreasonable to maintain that we may not retain anything in the English Church simply because it was to be found in the Roman Church previously. This reply by Whitgift was published in 1573, and called forth a Second Admonition, which is admitted to be from the pen of Thomas Cartwright, and in which he went over Whitgiff's argument point by point. The First Admonition having set forth what should be reformed, this points out how the work of reformation ought to be carried out. He suggests that a sufficient maintenance for the ministry should be provided so that every parish may have a preaching pastor; and that the statutes should be repealed which make the ministry partly to consist of lords spiritual, making one minister higher than another. For Christ most severely forbade His Apostles and successors all claims of primacy and dominion and gave an equal power and function to all the ministers of the Church. He suggests among other arrangements a series of ecclesiastical assemblies or conferences. "A conference," he says, "I call the meeting of some certain ministers and other brethren to confer and exercise themselves in prophesying or interpreting the Scriptures. At which conferences any one or any certain of the brethren are at the order of the whole to be employed upon some affairs of the Church; and where the demeanours of the ministers may be examined and rebuked." He further suggests the setting up of a synod provincial, that is, a meeting of certain of the consistory of every parish within a province, where great causes of the churches which could not be ended in their own consistories or conferences shall be heard and determined. From a provincial synod there might be an appeal to a national synod; and from this again to a more general synod of all churches.

From these larger arrangements he passes to the question of the local consistory which there should be in every congregation, consisting of the ministers and elders, or assistants whom the parish shall consent upon and choose, and upon whom, when chosen, the minister may lay his hands to testify to them their admission. The powers of the consistory were those of rebuke, and, if need arose, of excommunication. It was theirs also to abolish unprofitable ceremonies used in place of prayer, to put a stop to lewd customs either in games or otherwise, to exercise supervision over the relief of the poor, and to send representatives to a provincial or national council. He concludes with an appeal to the Queen, the council, the nobility and the commons to give the case a fair hearing or procure a free conference on the matter. The Queen especially is besought to take the defense of this movement upon her, and to fortify it by law. For though all orders should first of all be drawn from the Book of God, "yet it is her Majesty that by her princely authority should see every of these things put in practice, and punish those that neglect them."

In these two Admonitions addressed to Parliament we have what may be described as the Puritans' platform, the ecclesiastical system they would have brought about in England if they could. The effect they had upon the Queen was to excite her anger and to cause her to reprimand the bishops for not suppressing these men. Commissions were appointed under the Great Seal in every shire to put the penal laws into execution by way of Oyer and Terminer, and in the month of October she issued a proclamation requiring all offenders against the Act of Uniformity to be rigorously dealt with. Yet in spite of this, and about the same time, there were started certain voluntary associations which did much to prepare the minds of the people to look with favor upon the Puritan discipline. One of these was held in the town of Northampton and was not regarded as being contrary to the Act of Uniformity. Strype describes it as "a very commendable reformation instituted and established for Religion and good manners," and tells us that it was approved of by Dr. Scambler, the bishop of Peterborough. The ministers of the town, together with the mayor and the justices of the county met and agreed upon certain regulations for worship and discipline. Among other things it was decided that every Tuesday and Thursday there should be a lecture in the chief church of the town beginning with the confession and ending with prayer and a confession of faith; and that every Sunday evening the youth of the town should be instructed and examined in a portion of Calvin's Catechism. Altogether there were thirteen items in these arrangements, the last of which provided that excessive ringing of bells on the Lord's day should be prohibited, also the carrying of the bell before a corpse in the street, and bidding prayers for the dead.

Besides these voluntary associations, which were intended for the benefit of the laity, the clergy with the approval of the bishop set up a series of religious exercises which they called Prophesyings. This term took its rise from the passage in 1 Corinthians xiv. 31, "Ye may all prophecy one by one, that all may learn, and all be comforted." They were intended to advance the knowledge of the Scriptures among the clergy themselves, some of whom were but ill-instructed in sacred learning. They also conferred among themselves touching sound doctrine and good life and manners. There was a moderator appointed and three speakers, the first of whom after offering prayer should unfold a given passage of Scripture, set aside misapplications and then make a practical reflection, "but not dilate to a commonplace." The president should then call upon the rest of the brethren for their judgment on the matter. At a time when theological training was but little known we may well accept the judgment of Strype, the Church historian, on these gatherings when he calls the Prophesyings "a well-minded and religiously disposed combination of both bishop, magistrates and people, designed to stir up an emulation in the clergy to study the Scriptures, that they might be more capable of instructing the people in Christian knowledge."

Besides the county of Northampton these exercises were carried on also in the diocese of Norwich where they were regarded with favor by the bishop. But the Queen disliked them. They were not part of her arrangement for the Church, therefore not to be borne. Hearing that the discussions sometimes turned upon what was the scriptural form of church government, and that the laity had actually taken part in them, she sent peremptory orders to the archbishop to have them stopped. Parker communicated this order at once to Parkhurst, bishop of Norwich. But Parkhurst, who had been one of the protestant exiles himself in Mary's time, and had considerable sympathy with Puritan ideas, demurred. He said that the Prophesyings brought "singular benefit to the Church of God, as well in the clergy as in the laity, and was a right necessary exercise to be continued, so the same were not abused." One or two irregularities had prevailed but he had put a stop to them, "since which time he had not heard but all things had succeeded quietly, without offence to any." The archbishop chafed at this, and chafed still more when he discovered that the bishop of Norwich had communicated his order to certain members of the Privy Council and had received a letter from four members of that Council encouraging him to resistance. In this letter they say that having heard "that certain good exercises of Prophesying and expounding of Scriptures at Holt and other places in Norfolk whereby both Speakers and hearers do profit much in the knowledge of the Word of God…these are to require your Lordship, that so long as the Truth is godly and reverently uttered in this Prophesying, and that no seditious, heretical or schismatical doctrine can be proved to be taught, so good a help and means to true religion, may not be hindered and stayed, but may proceed and go forward to God's glory." But when the Queen heard of this interference with what was really her own command, an enquiry was made as to what their warrant was, Parker's biographer sums up the matter briefly telling us that another letter came from the archbishop to the bishop of Norwich which was followed immediately by one from the bishop of Norwich to the chancellor of his diocese, saying: "I am commanded by my Lord of Canterbury in the Queen her Majesty's name, that the Prophesyings throughout my diocese should be suppressed," and suppressed they were accordingly. The archbishop ended the correspondence by this caustic piece of advice:—"My Lord, be not you led by fantastical folk. Do not take such men to counsel, as, when they have endangered you, cannot bring you out of trouble. Of my care I have to you and to the Diocese I write thus much." This little episode lifts the veil for us for a moment from the inner working of the Church, making plain the fact that the supreme and shaping power was not the bishops, or the Privy Council or even the archbishop, but the great Tudor Queen whose dominion was absolute and whose will was law. Within eight months of the receipt of that letter Bishop Parkhurst went the way of all the earth, whither, in three months time, he was followed by the archbishop himself, upon which a further chapter in the history of Puritan Prophesyings is opened to us.

On the death of Parker, Archbishop Grindal was transferred from York to Canterbury. But the increase of dignity in his case meant increase of sorrow. He had done what he could to foster the Prophesyings and to keep them free from any cause of complaint in his northern province, intending to take the same course in that of Canterbury. This brought him into conflict with the Queen, who sent for him. She was informed, she said, that the rites and ceremonies of the Church were not duly observed in these prophesyings; that persons not lawfully called to be ministers exercised in them; these assemblies she maintained were illegal not being allowed by public authority; the laity neglected their business in going to these meetings; in short she commanded him peremptorily to put them down. It was good for the Church, she added, to have but few preachers, three or four in a county were quite sufficient. Now was he at a point, for he was painfully conscious of the need of enlightenment on the part of the people. When he went to his northern province he was appalled at their ignorance and superstition. The remains of the old Roman teaching were seen in their customs at the burial of the dead, and in their praying with beads. It seemed to him to be another religion, rather than that of the Reformed Church of England, which he found there. As Dr. Paget, the late bishop of Oxford, has well said: "It is easy to laugh at the Puritan exaltation of sermons, at their vehement denunciation of an unpreaching ministry; but it is unjust to forget the greatness and the persistence of the neglect which they denounced." Figures and formal documents from time to time show the strength of their case. In 1561 it was found that in the archdeaconry of London there were ministers who held three, some four, and one five, livings together. Strype reports that there was one minister who was vicar of St. Dunstan's West and held at the same time the following livings: Whiston and Doncaster in Yorkshire, Rugby in Warwickshire, and Barnet in Middlesex. And when, in 1586, the Puritans made a survey of the parishes they found in the 160 parishes of Cornwall only

29 preachers, in the 210 of Buckinghamshire only 30, in the 335 of Essex only 12; and altogether in 10,000 parish churches only 2000.

Such was the spiritual destitution of England at the time on the one side, and on the other, the resolute determination of the Queen to suppress those studies and exercises which in the archbishop's opinion might go some way in providing a remedy. As we gather, reading between the lines of his letter to the Queen dated December 20, 1576, she at their personal interview was passionate and stormful; "her speeches sounded very hardly against mine own person, exceedingly dismayed and discomforted me." He further implies that she would not listen to what he had to say in his own defense—"It was not your Majesty's pleasure then, to hear me at any length"; he therefore gave his answer in writing. After asserting his unchanging loyalty, and the absence of any desire on his part to offend her Majesty, he says it is only his duty to God which makes him refuse to suppress the preachers and the exercises. For public and continual preaching of God's word is the ordinary means and instrument of salvation of mankind; by this the glory of God is enlarged, faith is nourished and charity increased. He has been careful only to admit competent men to the office, no man professing either papistry or Puritanism, generally only graduates of the University, except some few who have excellent gifts of knowledge in the Scriptures, joined with good utterance and godly persuasion. He had himself within six years procured above forty learned preachers and graduates within the province of York besides those he found there. As to the Prophesyings, he has consulted other bishops who think as he does, that they are a thing profitable to the Church, and therefore expedient to be continued. He explains at length what was done at these gatherings and under what conditions, and gives his final determination thus: "I am forced with all humility, and yet plainly to profess that I cannot with safe conscience, and without the offence of the Majesty of God, give my assent to the suppressing of the said exercises. If it be your Majesty's pleasure to remove me out of this place, I will in all humility yield thereunto, and render again to your Majesty that I received of the same. He who acts against his conscience builds for hell. And what should I win, if I gained (I will not say a bishopric, but) the whole world, and lose mine own soul?"

The proud Tudor spirit of Elizabeth resented the faithfulness of this English Ambrose. Offended at this plain speaking she resolved to have him suspended and sequestered. As though she were archbishop herself, setting him aside, she sent her own commandment by her letters direct to the rest of the bishops, to put down these exercises. From that hour to the day of his death, seven years later, so far as his office as archbishop was concerned, he was practically a dead man. He was confined to his own house and sequestered for six months. Members of the Privy Council pleaded for him, and the bishops of his province besought his restoration to office, but in vain. At the end of the six months he was summoned before the Star Chamber, and there lectured and humiliated for his disobedience. He still remained sequestered and the duties of his office were placed in commission. There was some talk of actual deprivation, but stopping short of this he remained under the Queen's displeasure for the rest of his days. As these seven years passed slowly away, blindness came down upon the old man, and, tormented as he was besides by a painful disease, he sighed for that release which came at length on the 6th of July, 1583, in his seventy-third year. The Queen's despotic treatment of the highest ecclesiastical officer in the State is the most striking illustration of that absolute dominion she exercised always over the Church and by which she made it what it has since remained.

CHAPTER IV

PRESBYTERY *in* EPISCOPACY

The succession of Whitgift to Grindal in 1583, as archbishop of Canterbury, had much to do with the deepening and embitterment of the Puritan conflict within the Church's borders. The earlier bishops of Elizabeth's reign, Grindal, Parkhurst of Norwich, Jewell of Salisbury, Pilkington of Durham, Sandys of London, Horn of Winchester, and Cox of Ely, were not unfriendly to Puritan ideas, indeed, had the Queen permitted, would have made large concessions to them. For, as we know, they had themselves been exiles for protestantism among the Reformed Churches of Switzerland and the Upper Rhine. The advent of Whitgift to Canterbury, of

Aylmer to London and Freke to Norwich, meant more than an ordinary change in the episcopate. It meant that the Queen had now those to her hand who would readily work her will. There was a time when it seemed as if Whitgift would have thrown in his lot with the Puritan party. For in 1565, as fellow of Trinity and Lady Margaret professor he signed the petition to the chancellor against the revival of the papal vestments. But when in 1569 Cartwright created a stir in the University by assailing the hierarchical constitution of the Church, he at once entered the lists against him, reported his teachings to the chancellor, and joined the movement for obtaining new statutes, under the powers of which Cartwright was deprived of his Lectureship and expelled the University. In 1571, again, he was chosen to reply to the First Admonition of Field and Wilcocks, and also to the Second by Cartwright.

Thus when Whitgift came to be archbishop he was already in full sympathy with the Queen in her dislike of Puritan ideas. He was with her also in her love of pomp and stately show. No ecclesiastic since Cardinal Wolsey had departed so far from Puritan simplicity of life. Sir George Paule, the comptroller of his household, tells us that "he had a desire always to keep a great and bountiful House," that "upon some chief Festival days he was served with great solemnity upon the knee for the upholding of the state that belonged unto his place." He relates also how that "at his first journey into Kent he rode to Dover being attended by at least a hundred of his own servants in livery, whereof there were forty gentlemen in chains of gold." He further tells us that as every third year he rode into Kent he was not only attended by his own train of two hundred persons, but also with the gentlemen of the county, so "that he did sometimes ride into the city of Canterbury and into other towns with eight hundred or a thousand Horse."

On his advancement to his new position the Queen charged him to restore the discipline of the Church and the Uniformity established by law which, said she, "through the connivance of some prelates, the obstinacy of the Puritans and the power of some noblemen is run out of square." He readily fell into line with the royal wishes. The week after his confirmation at Lambeth he issued to the bishops of his province certain Articles which were aimed both against recusants and Puritans. Those specially bearing upon the latter required, (1) That none be permitted to read and preach and catechize in the Church unless he do, four times a year at least, minister the sacraments according to the Book of Common Prayer; (2) That all preachers do at all times wear and use such kind of apparel as is prescribed by the Book of Advertisements and her Majesty's Injunctions; and (3) That none be admitted unless he subscribe Articles (a) asserting the Queen's supremacy over all causes ecclesiastical as well as civil; (*b*) declaring that the Book of Common Prayer contains nothing contrary to the Word of God, he promising to use no other form of service; and (*c*) avowing acceptance of the Thirty-nine Articles of 1562.

After the promulgation of these Articles the archbishop carried out a Metropolitical Visitation to see them enforced. The first appearance of serious opposition was in his own diocese of Kent where some twenty ministers refused to subscribe. They were willing, they said, to subscribe to the Prayer Book, so far as it was not contrary to the Word of God, but they were not prepared to say there was nothing in the book contrary thereto, and they proceeded to indicate several things they regarded as imperfect. They also stated their objections to the observance of Saints' Days, and to the public reading of the Apocrypha, and they desired that the attire of ministers might be as in the second year of Edward VI. They further thought that the length of the Litany unduly hindered the sermon, that the prayers were over long, and they could not agree that children were really regenerated and necessarily saved by being baptized. On matters of church polity also they held equally decided views, objecting to the creation of superior clergy, and contending that archbishops, bishops and priests were inventions of men, the practical effect of which was to deface the true Word of God. They noted the omission of Elders such as those recognized in the New Testament, and contended that the people in every church ought to have right and liberty to choose their own ministers. Notwithstanding this statement of their views, however, they were still called upon to subscribe the new Articles, and refusing to do so, were pronounced contumacious, and required to answer at law in February following.

The same proceedings occurred elsewhere. In Norfolk alone, 64 parish ministers were suspended, and in Suffolk 60. In the six counties of Norfolk, Suffolk, Essex, Kent, Lincoln and Sussex, no fewer than 233 of the clergy were placed under interdict; those in Kent making formal appeal to the Privy Council against the archbishop's decision. There was also another part of his administration against which serious protest was made. In December, 1583, he established in more permanent and oppressive form the Court of High Commission, whose methods of investigation were described as worthy only of the Spanish Inquisition. A man might be called before this Court, without a charge and without an accuser, and there have the Oath *ex officio* administered to him, compelling him to reveal whatsoever he knew, whether of himself or anyone else. If he refused the oath he was at once committed to prison, simply for refusing. The names are given of twenty-five men confined in the gaols of London for ecclesiastical offences, who were there without warrant, and for months together without trial. They were treated as convicted criminals, were sometimes cruelly beaten and cast into "Little Ease," and some of them died in prison. This Court went on its evil way for half a century and more. It trespassed on competing jurisdictions, became in time one of the chief engines of Archbishop Laud's oppressions, and lasting on till the Long Parliament, was finally abolished by an Act with this ignominious clause—"that no such jurisdiction should be revived for the future in any Court whatsoever."

The year after the enlargement of the powers of the High Commission a series of searching Interrogatories was drawn up at Lambeth for the purpose of ascertaining how far the clergy were, or were not, obedient to the Act of Uniformity. They were twenty-four in all, covered every conceivable aspect of church life, and were so minute that it was next to impossible for a man to escape censure or conviction. Several of the clergy brought these questions to the notice of the Lord Treasurer whom they had come to look upon as their friend. At once he wrote to the archbishop protesting: "I have read these Articles of Enquiry," he said, "and find them so curiously penned, so full of branches and circumstances, as I think the Inquisition of Spain use not so many questions to comprehend and entrap their preyes... My good Lord, bear with my scribbling. I desire the peace of the Church. I desire concord and unity in the exercise of our

Religion. According to my simple judgement this kind of proceeding savours too much of the Romish Inquisition, and is rather a device to seek for offenders than to reform any."

While the archbishop was thus enforcing subscription and multiplying Interrogatories against the Puritans, they on their part were preparing to carry out more effectually a plan of campaign for securing the changes and reforms they deemed to be so needful for the spiritual welfare of the Church. They had no intention of separating from the Church. That was far indeed from their purpose, which was rather to bring about from within such changes as would make its government conform more nearly to what they regarded as the Scriptural idea. According to Thomas Fuller their "grand design was to set up a discipline within a discipline, Presbytery in Episcopacy." The hierarchical system seemed to them to be foreign to New Testament teaching, and their object was to substitute a government of pastors and ruling elders for that of archbishops and bishops, chancellors and archdeacons; and also to organize the parishes of England into a connected system of presbyteries, synods, and assemblies provincial and general.

To us, after centuries of established episcopacy, this scheme of theirs would have seemed daring and impossible. But not so to them. They were within fifty years of the time when a far greater revolution had been

THOMAS FULLER

possible; when the English Church was first severed from the See of Rome, and its bishops from the authority of the pope. In the eyes of all Europe that was a tremendous step to take, yet it was taken. It was taken again on the Accession of Elizabeth, and in 1570 confirmed by her solemn and formal excommunication, and that of her clergy, by the Bull of Pope Pius V. So that though the bishops were still there, their allegiance to the pope was no more. Whence then did they derive their authority? It was certainly not from the Scriptures, for there bishop and presbyter were equivalent terms denoting equality of rank. And it is further to be specially noted that up to this time the claim of divine right for Episcopacy had not been even suggested, much less formulated. It was Dr. Bancroft, in his sermon at St. Paul's Cross in 1588, who first put forward this claim, and then rather as a counterclaim to that of the Presbyterians who asserted divine right for their system. And when it was put forward, even the archbishop himself said he wished he could believe it, which he evidently did not. To show the novelty of the claim, we find Lord Burleigh referring the matter to Dr. Hammond, chancellor of the diocese of London for his opinion. His reply under date November 4, 1588, has been preserved among the Cecil MSS. in which he says that the name of a bishop, as of an office having superiority over many churches is not to be found in the Scriptures, the names of *episcopus* and *presbyter* importing one function.

He concludes with these decisive words: "The Bysshopps of our realm do not (so farre as I ever yet hearde), nor may not, clayme to themselves any other authorytie than is geeven them by the statute of the 25 of Kynge Henry the 8, recited in the fyrst yeare of her Majesty's raygne, neither is it reasonable they should make other clayme, for if it had pleased her Majesty, with the wysdome of the realme to have used no bysshopps at all, we could not have complayned justly of any defect in our Churche." If such were the views of leading churchmen at that time, it is not surprising if men with Puritan ideas felt themselves justified in thinking that ruling elders or presbyters might be substituted for bishops without any great violation of the spiritual order of the universe. Moreover the Church of England, since the Reformation, had regarded the Reformed Churches of the Continent as Sister Churches, and *they* had no bishops. And, what was still more to the purpose, Scotland also, under the influence of John Knox, had quite recently set aside episcopacy altogether, and established presbyterianism as the national form of church government.

These were weighty considerations, "but," to quote the earnest words of Dr. Paget, the late bishop of Oxford, "nothing surely, can have contributed so much to the opportunities, the power, the zeal, the hopes of Puritans as did the neglect of duty in the Church. At such a time ignorance and inability among the clergy were serious enough, but avarice and plain indifference to the meaning of a spiritual change were far worse." There was many "a parish whose minister could only struggle through the service, never preached, but read, perhaps four purchased sermons in the course of the year, or, it may be, had never resided in the place at all, and, had he done so, might only have made matters worse by the example of his vicious life."

It will be remembered that the Puritan scheme had been set forth by Field and Wilcocks in the First Admonition to Parliament of 1572. Two years later there appeared a yet more important and scholarly treatise, the famous *Ecclesiasticae Disciplinae et Anglicanae Ecclesiae... explicatio*. This work was first printed anonymously at Rochelle, a city which after the Huguenot Massacre of 1572 became the chief rendezvous of the French protestants, and where freedom of worship had been secured by treaty. Though issued without author's name it was known to be the production of Walter Travers, a fellow of Trinity, who after residing abroad became domestic chaplain to Lord Burghley and tutor to his son Robert Cecil. In 1581, on his lordship's recommendation he was appointed Afternoon Lecturer at the Temple Church, and by arrangement of the Benchers remained in this position after Richard Hooker was appointed Master. The writer of Hooker's Life reports that the morning sermon spoke the language of Canterbury, the afternoon that of Geneva. The church was crowded by lawyers deeply interested in the controversy, and, as Thomas Fuller tells us, "Some say the congregation ebbed in the morning and flowed in the afternoon," till a prohibition was served upon Travers in 1586. This man, then, was the author of the *Ecclesiastica Disciplina*, the most memorable book on the Puritan side. It originally appeared in 1574 in two forms, Latin and English, and a second edition of the English translation was printed in Geneva in 1580. The more important and conspicuous issue of the book, however, was in 1584, the year of Whitgift's Articles and Interrogatories. In that year, after more than fifty years of abeyance, the Cambridge University Press was reestablished, and one of its earliest issues was a revised English version of this treatise by Travers. On this Whitgift took alarm and on the 30th of June wrote to the chancellor in earnest remonstrance. "Ever since they had a Printing Press in Cambridge he greatly feared," he said, "that this and such inconveniences would follow." At his instigation the greater part of the printed impression was seized and destroyed. Still to some extent the book got into circulation and apart from its importance as the Puritan manifesto, from a literary point of view it has historical significance as being the treatise to which Hooker's great work on Ecclesiastical Polity was written as a reply.

The purpose of Travers was to discuss the proper

calling, conduct, knowledge, apparel and maintenance of a minister of religion; the offices of the doctor or teacher, the bishops, pastors and elders, and also the functions of the consistory. He began by showing the interdependence of doctrine and discipline. The danger of the Church of England, he maintained, was that doctrine was severed from discipline, and as a consequence the reformation thus far effected was incomplete and insecure; discipline being left unreformed, the reform of doctrine was precarious. What was needed now, therefore, was a new reformation dealing with the discipline of the Church. And the first thing to be done was to make a clean sweep of the Canon Law out of which (as out of a Trojan horse) have come archbishops, lord bishops, chancellors, archdeacons and the like, by whom the Church has been taken and enslaved. This accomplished, then let the true and right discipline be established, based upon the one essential principle of Puritanism which is that the Word of God is to be the authority, and that nothing be admitted save what can be confirmed by the voice and witness of God Himself.

This manifesto was issued from the Cambridge Press in the early summer of 1584, and on the 23rd of November following, Parliament again met for the dispatch of business. The Puritans were still sanguine of obtaining some advance in the practical achievement of their ideals, for in the House of Commons as well as in the

Privy Council there was a strong element in their favor. Their agents, Fuller tells us, were about the doors of the House all day, and making interest in the chambers of parliament men in the evening. On the 14th of December, three petitions were presented to the House, for liberty to godly preachers, restoration to office of those set aside, and for a speedy supply of able men for destitute parishes. At this point Dr. Turner rose and reminded the members of a Bill and a Book he on a former occasion had offered to the House: the Bill providing that no other form of subscription be required of ministers than that enjoined by the Act of 1571, and that no man presented by the lawful patron should be refused institution by the bishop except for obstinately defending heresies condemned by the Word of God. The Book offered along with the Bill consisted of thirty-four Articles, which by the advice of ministers had been reduced to sixteen, and these he desired might be submitted to the House of Lords and they be requested to join the Commons in exhibiting them in humble suit to the Queen. These sixteen Articles, presented in the form of a petition, were against insufficient ministers; in favor of parishes trying and allowing their pastors; against ministers being called to account by commissioners and officials instead of by the bishops themselves; in favor of six ministers being associated with the bishop in every ordination; for the restoration of deprived ministers; against excommunications *ex officio mero;* for permission to hold religious exercises and conferences in every archdeaconry under direction of the bishop; and for the removal of all non-residences and pluralities from the Church.

With some alterations and omissions this Book of Petitions was committed and approved, and was, soon after, presented by the Commons to the Lords. The answer of the Lords, as reported to the Lower House by Sir Francis Knollys, was to the effect that many of the Articles were regarded as unnecessary and others of them were already provided for; and as to the uniformity of Common Prayer which the petitioners wished to be left to the discretion of the minister, that had been established by Parliament. Both the archbishops spoke against the petition, and both also afterwards gave their reasons at length in writing.

This appeal being without effect, the Commons introduced other bills, among them being one against pluralities and non-residence, and one in favor of the right of appeal from the Ecclesiastical Courts to a higher tribunal. These passed the Lower House but were opposed and lost in the Lords. Undeterred by this additional defeat, the Commons resumed debate on certain other Bills intended to limit the power of the spiritual courts and also the jurisdiction of the prelates. Archbishop Whitgift, alarmed by the passing of two of these, wrote at once to the Queen informing her that, notwithstanding her recent charge to the Commons forbidding discussion on matters relating to religion, they had passed one Bill relating to the ministry, and another giving liberty to marry at all times of the year, contrary to the ancient Canons. At once a message came from the Queen to the Commons reprimanding them for thus encroaching on her supremacy, and commanding the Speaker "to see that no Bills concerning Reformation in Ecclesiastical Causes be exhibited, and should they be exhibited that they be not read."

Still, in spite of this remonstrance, the Commons introduced a Bill for further reformation, and what was more, connected with the Bill a proposed form of service entitled "A Booke of the Forme of Common Prayers, Administration of the Sacraments, etc., agreeable to God's Worde, and the Use of the Reformed Churches," which it was proposed to substitute for the one already in use. On motion being made for the reading of this book the speaker reminded them that the Queen had already commanded the House not to meddle with such matters, since she herself had promised to take order therein, he therefore advised them to refrain. This raised a storm, and the House being still resolved to have the book read, the speaker rose and more decisively declared such reading to be out of order, the book prescribing a new form of administration to the discredit of the Book of Common Prayer. It could only have the effect of rousing her

Majesty's indignation against them. Therein he rightly judged, for though the book was not read, but only proposed to be, the Queen sent a message demanding both the petition and the book, and ordering such of the members as had shown zeal in the matter to be sent prisoners to the Tower. Nor was this all. In her speech, when dismissing Parliament at the end of the session, she returned to this interference with her prerogative, as she regarded it. There was one thing, she said, that touched her so near that she might not overskip, namely, religion. To find fault with the order of the clergy was virtually to slander both her and the Church whose overlooker she was. If schisms or errors heretical were suffered the negligence would be hers, and could not be excused. After charging the bishops, she turned to those who were bent on further reformation, saying that she saw many overbold with God Almighty, making too many scannings of His blessed Will, as lawyers did with human testaments. This presumption was so great that she might not suffer it. She was minded neither to animate Romanists nor tolerate new-fangleness, but to guide both by God's true rule. Such was the Queen's determination, and it was the memory of such interference with the liberties of Parliament as these that led Hume the historian, who had no great liking for Puritans, to say: "So absolute indeed was the authority of the Crown that the precious spark of liberty had been *kindled* and was *preserved* by the

Puritans *alone*; and it was to this sect that the English owe the whole freedom of their constitution."

Finding that nothing was to be looked for from appeals to Parliament, the Puritan clergy within the Church resolved to take steps themselves for a practical carrying out of the church discipline they held to be more scriptural. As early as 1572, in the November after the Bartholomew Massacre in Paris of the previous August, they had set up a congregation after the presbyterian model at Wandsworth, then a mere village on the banks of the Thames. Some fifteen ministers from London and from the neighborhood of Wandsworth were the leaders of this movement, there being associated with them a considerable number of influential laymen. At their meeting on the 20th of November eleven elders, or presbyters, were chosen and their orders described as "the Orders of Wandsworth." This organization has sometimes been described as the first presbyterian church in England. Strictly speaking, however, it was rather an association within the borders of the Established Church than an organized separation from it. The proceedings of this community were carried on with great secrecy, so much so that though the commissioners knew of its existence they were unable to find out who belonged to it. Besides this organized movement at Wandsworth, separate communities were established for the observance of the Lord's Supper, those joining in them signing a common declaration to the effect that they wished to unite themselves in prayer and hearing with those who renounced the idolatries of the Church, notwithstanding the danger incurred by not coming to their own parish churches. Each of those who signed also personally assented to these solemn words: "Having joined myself to the Church of Christ I have yielded myself to the discipline of God's Word which, if I again forsake, I should be forsaking the Union wherein I am knit to the body of Christ."

In 1575 a step forward was taken by the establishment of the presbyterian discipline in the Channel Islands. After the massacre in Paris in 1572 many French protestants fled to these islands for safety, and were, by the lords of the council, allowed to retain the Genevan or French form of service to which they had been accustomed. Representatives from various districts met at St. Peter's Port, Guernsey, when the draft of a form of church discipline was duly discussed and adapted to the use of the islands. This was agreed upon the following year at a synod held in Guernsey, June, 1576, and was afterwards confirmed at a later synod held in Jersey in October, 1577. Meantime the Puritans on the mainland kept up their Associations and private assemblies. The two counties of Warwick and Northampton were especially forward in the movement. An important meeting was held at Cockfield in Suffolk, when sixty ministers from Norfolk, Suffolk and Cambridgeshire came together in conference, to determine what in the use of the Prayer Book might be tolerated and what refused. This meeting stood adjourned to Cambridge at the next Commencement, and afterwards from thence to London. The result of these three synodical gatherings was embodied in certain conclusions, formally drawn up by Cartwright and Travers, the object of which was the introduction of important changes in the organization and worship of the National Church which should yet not mean separation from that Church. Churches were to be arranged in classical, provincial and national synods; ministers should be called to the pastorate, first of all, by the churches they were to serve, and this call be approved by the local classic meeting in conference; and then the minister, so called and so approved, should by letters be commended to the bishop for ordination. Churchwardens and collectors for the poor could be turned into elders and deacons without disturbing the present arrangement. In the matter of subscription to the Articles and Book of Common Prayer, if this should be again urged, it was decided that it might be consented to only in accordance with the statute of 1571 which limited subscription to such Articles only as contain the sum of the Christian faith and the doctrine of the Sacraments. Subscription to the Prayer Book and to the rest of the Articles should be resisted even though a man should be deprived of his ministry for refusing. Beyond these arrangements a more extended form of organization was also resolved upon. The shire of Northampton, for example, was arranged in three separate classes, held in the towns of Northampton, Daventry and Kettering. A provincial synod of these classes was also convened in the town of Northampton, and similar gatherings held in other counties, especially Warwickshire, Suffolk, Norfolk and Essex. It was further ordered that the results arrived at in these conferences should be reported to the greater assemblies held in Cambridge at the time of the Sturbridge Fair of 1587, and in London at the time of the Bartholomew Fair; such times were chosen as being occasions when considerable gatherings of people would be less noticeable. Reports were also to be sent up to a synod held at St. John's College, Cambridge, at the Sturbridge Fair time of 1589. On this occasion Travers's Discipline, after further revision and correction was subscribed to by the members present as essential and necessary for all time.

At the Northamptonshire Assembly an Ecclesiastical Survey of the churches of the county was ordered to be made and a return sent in of the value of each benefice and of the population of the parish, giving also the name of the incumbent and a description of his personal character and ministry. It was also resolved to obtain, if possible, a more extended, a national, survey of churches for parliamentary purposes, and to arrange for representatives to be sent up to London when Parliament was in session. It will thus be seen that there was a very businesslike air about this design for "setting up a discipline within a discipline, Presbytery in Episcopacy."

There was another department of their propaganda destined to play an important part in the movement. The men driven from their ministry and silenced from public speech began to defend themselves by means of the press. The age of that pamphleteering, which in the next century was to assume such portentous dimensions, had begun to dawn. Tracts and treatises appeared in quick succession in which the state of things existing in the Church was laid bare with no gentle hand, and strange tales became current talk. The archbishop decided all this must come to an end. On June 23, 1586, therefore, he obtained from the Star Chamber a decree for limiting the number of printing presses and for keeping under strict surveillance such as were licensed. It was ordered that no press should be set up outside the city and suburbs of London, except one in the University of Cambridge and one in the University of Oxford, one and no more. Even in London no printer might start business except with the consent of the wardens of the Company of Stationers, and presses everywhere were to be open and accessible at all times to the said wardens. Finally no book was to be printed till first read by the archbishop, the bishop of London, or by censors of their appointment.

Under the powers conferred by this decree, the printing office of Robert Waldegrave in St. Paul's Churchyard was broken open on April 16, 1588, by John Wolfe, the beadle of the Stationers' Company. The press was seized, the letters defaced and various printed sheets carried away. Among the latter were some copies of a work entitled *The State of the Church of England laid open in a Conference.* No name of the author appeared upon the title-page, but it is now known to have been the work of John Udall, the vicar of Kingston-on-Thames, a convinced Puritan, and a man of some reputation as an author and an eloquent preacher. This book of his, better known under the title of *Diotrephes*, though not belonging to the series, may yet be described as the precursor of the Martin Marprelate Tracts, so famous in the discussions of the time. This description of the state of the Church was brought out in the form of a dialogue which is supposed to have taken place at an Inn on the North Road where wayfarers from Scotland and the North met travelers from London and the South. In this conversation there are not a few Bunyanesque touches of humor, with suggestive asides, reminding us again and again of Mr. Byends and his way of looking at life. Diotrephes is a bishop travelling incognito from Scotland where, to his distress, the Puritans have set up their discipline and utterly overthrown the sovereignty of the bishops. He would know from the inn-keeper what news there is of church affairs hereabouts. This is not a subject on which mine host is very strong, for he seldom goes to church, but he will fetch in a money-lender from London who happens to be in the house. On this worthy being appealed to, he relates that the bishops—"God's blessing be on them for it—say pretty well by one and by one to these precise and whot preachers; for some of them are put to silence and others are close prisoners in the Gatehouse; some are well-loaden with irons in the White Lion, and some are in the Clinke." This is good news to the inn-keeper who likes not these precisian preachers. For one of that sort has come to this town, "a town that stands on victualling, being thorow-fare, and he preacheth against good-fellowship which he calls drunkenness," so that he has spoilt half their gains. At this point one Paule, a preacher from London joins in the talk, giving a searching account of church matters from the Puritan point of view, and, as we may suppose, there is animated discussion till bedtime. Next morning, before the travelers set forth on their various ways, the talk is renewed, the concluding part, which is the longest, being a conference between Tertullus a Catholic and Diotrephes as to how they can best combine to check-mate the Puritans and safeguard the bishops. They agree that it would be well to secure the lords of the council, and make sure of the universities, for they have great privileges and Puritans start up every day.

Even from this brief glimpse it will be seen that *Diotrephes* was fitting forerunner to "Martin Marprelate, Gentleman," and indeed was the work of the same printer who, six months later, sent forth *The Epistle*, the first of the Marprelate series. For Waldegrave, after having had press and types seized in London made his way to Kingston, Udall's town, and thence, to avoid observation, to East Molesey near by, and set up another press at which soon after midsummer 1588, he printed another book for Udall entitled *A Demonstration of Discipline*; this being followed in November by *The Epistle*. The appearance of the latter, being as we have said, the first of the Marprelate series produced a great sensation and became the talk of the town. "Every man," says Martin, "talks of my Worship; he says that he has been entertained at Court." This fame, naturally, was not without its peril; the authorities were soon eagerly in pursuit, and as East Molesey was no longer considered safe the press and types were secretly carted away to Fawsley, the seat of Sir Richard Knightley, near Northampton, and there *The Epitome*, the second Martin, which had been promised in *The Epistle*, was printed.

Early in 1589 Thomas, the bishop of Winchester, in reply to these attacks published an *Admonition to the People of England*, denying the charges made against the bishops and urging as a warning that this attack upon the Church would certainly be followed by an attack upon the State. Meantime to evade pursuit, the secret press was removed from Fawsley to Coventry where the broadside known as *The Minerals*, one of the minor Marprelate tracts, was printed in February. Towards the end of March another of the tracts was printed at Coventry having for its title, what was then a common street-cry, *Hay any Worke for the Cooper*, which of course was a rejoinder to Bishop Cooper's *Admonition*. After this issue Waldegrave was succeeded as printer by John Hodgkins. The press was again removed from place to place and at length, through the vigilance of the Earl of Derby, was seized at Newton, a mile or so out of Manchester, then one of the strongholds of Puritanism. Both press and printers were at once sent back to London under escort, the printers being received as close prisoners to Bridewell.

It does not fall within the purpose of this narrative to follow any further the history of these once-famous tracts. It may suffice to say that altogether there were seven of them, and that while their authorship, like that of the *Letters of Junius*, is one of the unsolved problems of literature, there is a growing consensus of opinion that they were mainly, if not entirely, from the pen of Job Throckmorton, the Puritan squire of Haseley Manor, near Warwick; and that along with Waldegrave and Hodgkins, John Penry was concerned with him in the arrangements for printing.

The purpose of the writer was to carry the war into

the camp of the men who, as he believed, were not only oppressing the Puritan clergy, but were themselves open to serious charges of neglect and worldliness. This he did, exposing them to ridicule by means of banter and satire. Yet it must be said that in the midst of all his banter, and under all his personalities Martin had a serious and earnest purpose, which can scarcely be said of the anti-Martinists, who, in their replies to his attacks, descended only too often to grossness and indecencies. But what we are now mainly concerned with is the fact that the Marprelate Tracts, with their compromising charges and irritating personalities, gave added force to the resentment roused by the persistent and organized attempts of the Puritan party to overthrow Episcopacy and to substitute for it the system of Scotland and Geneva in the government of the English Church.

We may now turn for a moment to see how these attempts, at length, reached a crisis and ended in conspicuous failure. It goes without saying that the authorities of the Church were not altogether ignorant of what was going on. For letters had been intercepted and plans laid bare; and at length on July 16, 1590, Archbishop Whitgift drew up a series of Articles against the leaders of the movement under which, later in the year, they were summoned before the Court of High Commission, and afterwards called to appear before the Star Chamber. Cartwright was summoned from his hospital at Warwick to London and lodged in the Fleet prison. He and his companions were examined again and again and refusing to take the oath *ex officio* were consigned to prison. There they lingered on all through the cold and wretchedness of that and the following winter without any farther process. After two years and more of this kind of experience they petitioned the Queen for a merciful release, repudiating the charges of sedition, schism and rebellion, which had been brought against them, and assuring her of their loyalty. But she was deaf to their pleading. Eventually Cartwright was released upon promise of quiet and peaceable behavior, but only upon bond to appear before the High Commission when called upon. Several of the prisoners yielded at length, took the oath and gave evidence as to what had taken place in their assemblies. Others still refused and remained under suspension, some for five and others for seven years. John Udall, whose *Diotrephes* and *Demonstration of Discipline* could neither be forgotten nor forgiven, was singled out for special indignity. As his vicarage was in the county of Surrey he was taken, heavily ironed, and indicted at the Croydon Assizes of July, 1590, for sedition, inasmuch as he "not having the fear of God before his eyes did maliciously publish a slanderous and infamous libel against the Queen's Majesty, her Crown and Dignity." So ran the indictment in which was also quoted an objectionable passage from the *Demonstration*, and reference made to the burning of his other book the *Diotrephes* dialogue. After the forms of law had been gone through the prisoner at the bar was convicted of felony, and condemned to be executed: any criticism of arrangements the Queen had set up in the Church being ruled to be sedition against her person. No immediate attempt, however, was made to carry out this, which has been described as an atrocious sentence, and Udall lingered on indefinitely in prison. We gather from records of the time that great resentment was felt at these proceedings, and that persons of influence, such as Sir Walter Raleigh, the Earl of Essex, and Nowell, the dean of St. Paul's, interested themselves in the case of this man and interceded on his behalf, but without result. Further still, in March, 1592, the Governor of the Turkey Company offered to send him to Syria, as pastor to their agents in that country, if he could be released at once. But he was not, and the vessel was under the necessity of sailing without him. Three months later a pardon was sealed in June, but even after this there were other requisite formalities, and before these could be gone through, the hardships of prison life had done their work, and John Udall died while still a prisoner in Southwark gaol.

CHAPTER V

ABSOLUTISM *and* LIBERTY

The sternly repressive measures carried out by Archbishop Whitgift against those who sought to graft the presbyterian discipline upon the episcopal system were successful in crushing out all further attempts at organization on presbyterian lines; but not the earnest desire after further reformation in a Puritan direction. Disaffection was not put an end to by being driven out of sight. Those who were locked up in the prisons of London represented only a fraction of those who were longing for change and more earnest spiritual life. The movement had spread widely in the English shires, and out of the two thousand ministers in the Church who were really preachers no fewer than five hundred subscribed the Book of Discipline in 1590, and prayed Parliament that this book "might be from henceforth authorised, put in use and practised through-out all Her Majesty's dominions." This was an ominous fact, and when Hooker in 1594 published the first four books of his *Ecclesiastical Polity*, he evidently felt that even then the threatening danger had not ceased to impend. In a long preface he explains why he entered upon this, the great work of his life—"though for no other cause yet for this: that posterity may know we have not loosely through silence permitted things to pass away as in a dream."

Having traced the course of the Puritan movement *within* the National Church from 1564 to 1590, we turn now to that other outworking of yet more strenuous Puritan feeling which took shape *outside* the State Church system, taking the form of Separatism and the establishment of self-governing churches. This movement took its rise mainly in two different centers—London and the Eastern Counties, the former being specially associated with the names of Henry Barrow and John Greenwood, the latter with that of Robert Browne. The last-named reformer, from whom came the name "Brownist," was born about 1550, the third son of Anthony Browne of Tolethorpe Manor, sheriff of Rutlandshire in 1546, 1558 and 1571. He graduated at Cambridge in 1572, and even as an undergraduate was spoken of as "being known and counted forward in religion." Moreover he was at the University at the time of the Puritan excitement caused by the vestment controversy and Cartwright's lectures. And after leaving Cambridge, "he fell into great care and was sore grieved while he long considered many things amiss, and the cause of all to be the woeful and lamentable state of the Church." In 1580, he had reached the theoretical position of Congregationalism, which is that you cannot accept the entire baptized population of a given parish as the Church of Christ in that place, for, as he expressed it, "the Kingdom of God is not to be begun by whole parishes but rather of the worthiest were they never so few." The spiritual few he would take as a nucleus and work from them as the centre. On this principle as the theoretical justification of separation, and not merely on dislike of ceremonies and prelatical power, he and his friend Richard Harrison, also a Cambridge man, organized a free church in Norwich in 1581. They also visited other places in East Anglia, notably Bury St. Edmunds, where there were "assemblies of the common people to the number of a hundred at a time, who met in private houses and conventicles." As a result Browne found himself in prison and on his release went to Middelburg in Zealand, where in 1582 he printed and published the three books in which he gave formal expression to the principles he had embraced. These were: *A Treatise of Reformation without tarying for anie; The life and manner of*

all true Christians; and A Treatise upon the 23. of Matthewe.
His friend Richard Harrison also published at the same
time a small book on the 122nd Psalm bearing in the
same direction. These books were conveyed over into
England secretly, and in June, 1583, a royal proclamation
was issued against them, commanding the destruction
of all copies of "the same or such like seditious books."
About the time this proclamation appeared, the Assizes
were held at Bury St. Edmunds, when John Copping and
Elias Thacker were convicted of sedition for spreading
these books, and were hanged before the Assizes were
over. About the same time also, and upon the same
charge, William Denys was hanged at Thetford, criticism
of the Queen's Church being ruled to be sedition
against the Queen's person.

Earlier even than this Eastern movement in the
direction of Separatism, was another which was organized
in London some time before 1571. Three documents
which happen to have been preserved together among
the State Papers bring to our notice what would seem
to have been the earliest organized Congregational
church after the Reformation. The most important of the
three is a petition to the Queen signed by twenty-seven
persons, one of them giving Whitechapel Street as an
address, urging the necessity of ecclesiastical reform.
They describe themselves as "We a poor congregation
whom God hath separated from the Church of England

and from the mingled and false worshipping therein" and say that "as God giveth strength at this day we do serve the Lord every Sabbath day in houses, and on the fourth day come together weekly to use prayer and exercise discipline on them that do deserve it, by the strength and true warrant of the Lord God's Word." They farther state incidentally that the maintainers of the Canon Law have "by long imprisonment pined and killed the Lord's servants, as our minister Richard Fitz, Thomas Bowland, deacon, one Partryche and Gyles Fouler, and besides them a great multitude." Along with this written and subscribed petition there is a small printed sheet in black letter entitled *The trewe Markes of Christ's Church &c.* These are three (1) the glorious Word and evangel are preached freely and purely; (2) the sacraments are administered according to the institution and good word of the Lord Jesus; and (3) discipline is administered agreeably to the same heavenly and almighty word. The third document, also in black letter, sets forth reasons for separation from the Anglican Church and prays that "God may give them strength still to strive in suffering under the Cross, that the blessed Word of our God alone may rule and have the highest place." What became of this little community we do not know. It was probably broken up and scattered, the members of it being sent to prison, and these somewhat pathetic and time-worn documents preserved in the Record Office are all that remains to tell the tale. But moving westward from Whitechapel in 1571, we come in later years upon congregations of Separatists meeting in various places in the city, and in the woods of Islington where the protestants were accustomed to meet for secret worship in Queen Mary's time. On Sunday, October 8, 1586, twenty-one of these people were met at Henry Martin's house in the parish of St. Andrew's-in-the-Wardrobe, and, as they were listening to the reading of the Scriptures by John Greenwood, they were broken in upon by the bishop of London's pursuivants and brought as prisoners the same day to his palace at Fulham for examination. In the event ten were released and eleven kept close prisoners; of the eleven thus detained Alice Roe and Margaret Maynard died of the "infection" of Newgate, and John Chandler, and Nicholas Crane, an aged man of sixty-six years, also died in prison.

John Greenwood, who was reading the Scriptures to these people at the time they were broken in upon, was, like Robert Browne, an undergraduate at Cambridge at the time of the Cartwright controversy. His mind was so powerfully influenced by this that even after he had left the University and had received ordination he first resigned his cure, then a private chaplaincy held in the house of Lord Rich of Rochford, and finally left the Episcopal Church altogether. About the same time he formed an intimate friendship with Henry Barrow, the son of a country squire of Shipdam in Norfolk, he being a kinsman also of Lord Bacon. At the close of his Cambridge career, Barrow was trained for the bar at Gray's Inn, living in London for a while. Turning casually into a church one day he heard a sermon which resulted in a changed life for him. It became whispered among his acquaintances that Barrow had turned Puritan, or as Bacon described it: "He made a leap from a vain and libertine youth to a preciseness in the highest degree." Changed life brought changed companionships and he and John Greenwood became from this time friends of the most intimate kind. When therefore Greenwood had been arrested in London and sent prisoner to the Clink, Barrow went to visit him on Sunday morning, November 19, 1586. Little knowing that he was already suspect because of his ecclesiastical opinions, he found that he had walked into a trap, for they had been on the lookout for him. He was arrested at once and sent in a boat up the river to Lambeth, where he was examined by Whitgift and committed to the Gatehouse. Five months later he was again examined before the Court of High Commission; and at the Newgate Sessions of May, 1587, he and his friend Greenwood were indicted under the Act of 1581, for "withdrawing from the religion now by her Highness's authority established," and committed to the Fleet prison.

During the long and weary years of imprisonment

which followed between his committal to the Fleet in May, 1587, and his execution at Tyburn in March, 1593, Barrow produced the books with which his name is associated, the sheets of which were conveyed out of prison secretly as he wrote them, and printed abroad at Dort by one Hanse. The central principle he insists upon in these books is that which Browne had enunciated before him, namely, that you cannot have a truly Christian Church unless it is composed of spiritual men: "a true planted and rightly established Church of Christ is a company of faithful people, separated from unbelievers, gathered in the name of Christ whom they truly worship and readily obey. They are a brotherhood, a communion of saints, each one of them standing in and for their Christian liberty to practise whatsoever God hath commanded and revealed unto them in His holy Word." That Word and not Tradition is to be their guide; that is the golden reed for measuring our temple, our altar and our worship. He is opposed to all hierarchies in the Church, to all lords and rulers except Christ Himself. According to him the greatest Elder of the Church, the pastor, is but a servant and steward of the house, not lord of the heritage; his honor consists in his service, and his service belongs unto all. A Church constituted of spiritually renewed men and recognizing the headship and authority of Christ is capable of self-government, has right and power to discipline itself, having, as every particular congregation the power of our Lord Jesus Christ to censure sin and excommunicate obstinate offenders.

Such were Barrow's views on Church government, which were essentially and fundamentally opposed to the Established Church system which lodged that government in the hands of Queen and Privy Council, archbishops, bishops and archdeacons, and in a Star Chamber and Court of High Commission. The books in which he had promulgated these views, and which he had composed stealthily during his long imprisonment, were now regarded as a further, an additional offence against the Queen's supremacy in things ecclesiastical as well as civil. For this further offence he was brought to trial on the 11th of March, 1593, and on the 23rd both he and John Greenwood were convicted of publishing seditious books and sentenced to death for the offence.

Writing to a lady of rank, a kinswoman of his own, between condemnation and execution, Barrow says: "For books written more than three years since (after well near six years' imprisonment) the prelates have caused us to be indicted, arraigned, condemned." On March 24, the morning after sentence had been passed preparations were made for execution; Barrow and Greenwood were brought out of prison, their irons smitten off and they were on the point of being bound to the cart when a reprieve came. A few days later, however, they were early and secretly conveyed along Holborn to the place of execution at Tyburn; they were actually tied by the neck to the fatal tree and were speaking a few parting words to the people when again a reprieve came; "the people with exceeding rejoicing and applause" cheering them on their way back to prison. Finally, on the 6th of April, they were again conveyed to the place of execution and this time they returned no more. The following month, on the 29th of May, John Penry, who had recently gone over from presbyterianism to separatism, was led out to St. Thomas-a-Watering, Kennington, and there hanged also, at a time when few were near. Thus the three Martyrs of 1583 in the Eastern Counties were followed by the three of 1593 in London and the roll was complete. Meantime, while these trials and executions were going forward, the Parliament of 35 Elizabeth was in session from February 19 to April 10, when a measure was passed, the stern Conventicle Act of 1593, which was intended to crush Nonconformity once for all, so far as Separatism was concerned. This Act, which was the culmination of the measures taken by Elizabeth to repress Puritanism, provided that if any person above the age of sixteen years should refrain, or persuade any other person to refrain, from coming to Church for one month without lawful cause, or be present at any assemblies, conventicles or meetings under color or pretence of any exercise of religion, such person shall be committed to prison there to remain without bail or mainprise until they shall conform and yield themselves to come to some Church according to her Majesty's laws and statutes aforesaid. It was further provided that if such persons did not conform and make public confession and submission in the parish church they shall abjure this realm of England and all others the Queen's Majesty's dominions forever; and if they returned without special license, in every such case, the person so offending should be adjudged a felon, and should suffer as in case of felony, without benefit of clergy. Under the provisions of this Act it will be seen that those of the Puritans who were Separatists had no choice but either to conform or go into exile. Penry before his execution had advised his London brethren to choose the latter: "Seeing banishment, with loss of goods is likely to betide you all, prepare yourselves for this hard entreaty." He advises them to go and to keep together, not leaving the poor and friendless to stay behind and be forced to break a good conscience for want of support and kindness; and especially in pathetic entreaty he beseeches them to take his poor and desolate widow and his fatherless and friendless orphans with them into exile whithersoever they went. This they did when many of them in the summer and autumn of that year went over into Holland. For in the Netherlands Republic there was, what there was not in England, liberty of conscience and freedom of worship. On the 5th of July, 1581, the knights, nobles and cities of Holland and Zealand had called upon William

JAMES I

the Silent to accept entire authority as sovereign and chief of the land, directing him "to maintain the exercise only of the Reformed Evangelical religion, without, however, permitting that enquiries should be made into any man's belief or conscience, or that any injury or hindrance should be offered to any man on account of his religion." Thus Amsterdam became the asylum of liberty, and drew to itself from many lands those who valued freedom, civil or religious. Among these were the members of the Separatist Church in London, also those who went over from Gainsborough and Scrooby, the last-named community, after remaining some months at Amsterdam, ultimately settling at Leyden where they remained till 1620, when they sailed in the *Mayflower* for New England. These Churches seeking refuge in Holland between 1595 and 1620, were recruited by other exiles for conscience sake from various parts of England. As we gather from the Puiboeken, or public records of their adopted country, these came from no fewer than twenty-nine English counties, besides the Welsh county of Caermarthen. Northumberland and Yorkshire were represented, so were Sussex and Kent; Cornwall and Devon sent of their people as did also Norfolk and Suffolk; the North and South Midlands as well as Lancashire and Lincoln.

During the last three or four years of Elizabeth's life there was a kind of truce between the Church and the Puritans. It was known that King James would, in the event of the death of the Queen, who was now advanced in years, succeed to the English throne, and as he had been brought up among the presbyterians of Scotland, changes might be imminent. The Puritans were hopeful of his favor, and when he did succeed and was on his way to London, they met him at Hinchinbrook and presented what was called the Millenary Petition, as being supposed to be signed by a thousand of the English Puritan clergy, pleading for further reforms in the Puritan direction. Nothing came of this, however, and the result of the Hampton Court Conference was equally disappointing. The King let them state their case and then bluntly told them that if that was all they had to say they must either conform or go. Subscription to the whole Prayer Book and Articles, which was the special achievement of Elizabeth's reign, was still to be enforced; and to this were to be added the Canons made by Convocation of 1604, which were to be the contribution to Church order to signalize the reign of James. Some of these canons were old and some were new. They asserted again the Church of England to be the true and Catholic Church of this realm, and any one denying this would be *ipso facto* excommunicate; so would all objectors to the Prayer Book, and those who said that the government of the Church by archbishops and bishops was repugnant to the Word of God. And in those days excommunication meant more than spiritual deprivation. It meant that he who was subjected to that penalty must not merely be turned out of the congregation of the faithful, but as a citizen would be rendered incapable of suing for his lawful debts, and be liable to be imprisoned for life by process of the civil courts, or until reconciled to the Church; and when he died would be degradingly denied Christian burial. Bancroft, who on the death of Whitgift had succeeded to the See of Canterbury, showed no lack of zeal in enforcing these canons. He renewed the use of copes, surplices, caps and hoods, according to the *first* Service Book of Edward VI, and he obliged the clergy to subscribe over again the three Articles of Whitgift, which by Canon XXXVI they were to declare they did "willingly and from the heart." As the result of this further action more than 300 ministers were silenced or deprived, some by excommunication, and others by being forced to leave the country and go into banishment.

But note must now be taken of the fact that James summoned a new Parliament in January, and Parliament under James proved to be more independent than it had dared to be under Elizabeth. Before granting supplies they first demanded redress of grievances, and further claimed the privileges of the Commons of England not as a matter of grace, but as their lawful inheritance. It soon became clear that a new era had dawned. Elizabeth even had scarcely been able to restrain Parliament from debating the subject of the state of the Church of England, James could not restrain them at all. For a majority of the Commons were Puritans, not in the sense of those of a later time who were opposed on principle to government by bishops and to the use of the Book of Common Prayer, but in the sense that they wished that men who had scruples of conscience should be allowed some latitude, and they were of opinion that it was of more importance to secure effective preachers and a resident clergy, than to contend for a rigid observance of form and ceremony. Bills for providing a learned and godly ministry and for abating pluralities were brought in and passed by the Commons, but were thrown out in the Lords. On May 30, the King came down to Parliament and rebuked the Commons for intrusion upon his prerogative, as Elizabeth would have done, but he was not met as she was. They were not willing to acknowledge that they had exceeded their powers. On the contrary, in respectful terms they asserted that their privileges were their due inheritance no less than their lands and goods, and further declared that these privileges had been more dangerously impugned than at any former time, their freedom of speech impaired by many reproofs, and their House made contemptible in the eyes of the world. As to the Church they expressly denied the power of the Crown to "alter religion" or to make any law concerning it otherwise than by consent of Parliament. This theory of government ran directly counter to that held by the King, who claimed that kingly power admitted of no restraint by law. Here were two opposing theories admitting of no reconciliation; and Parliament placed theirs on record in strenuous and unmistakable language: "The prerogatives of princes," said they, "may easily and do daily grow: the privileges of subjects are, for the most part, at an everlasting stand, and being once lost are not recovered but with much disquiet." It has been well said that this which had been the history of France, of Castile, of Aragon, and of other continental kingdoms might have been the history of England. Absolute monarchies had elsewhere risen on the ruins of national liberties, and this might have been the fate of England too but for the patriotic spirit of her statesmen. Said a parliamentary orator in 1625: "We are the last monarchy in Christendom that maintains its rights."

In this great and far-reaching controversy the nation at large had to choose sides as to whether Church and State should be controlled by the representatives of the people or by the will of the King. The choice was made. Convocation adopted the principle that resistance to the Sovereign is in all cases condemned by the law of God. Church and King joined hands on the doctrine of passive obedience and non-resistance; the Puritans and Parliament in maintaining the principles of constitutional government. In this fateful severance there was involved the history of the coming time, the origin of contending parties in the State, the outbreak of Civil War and the consequent downfall of the hierarchical constitution of the Church.

Charles I succeeded to the throne of England on the death of his father in 1625, and in one dangerous direction proceeded to tread in his steps. James, when refused supplies by Parliament until after redress of grievances, resorted again and again to unconstitutional methods of obtaining the money he needed for his wars. He imposed taxes on imports by his own authority; these impositions being chiefly laid on articles of luxury or on foreign manufactures which competed with native industry. Later on he asked for loans, and then sought for benevolences. Letters were written to every county and borough asking for voluntary gifts for the needs of the King, but at the end of two months only £500 was subscribed in reply, and after two years of continuous pressure only £66,000 had been raised altogether. King Charles, his son and successor, when he came to the throne travelled along the same unconstitutional road, with this difference only that he travelled faster and farther. Without authority of Parliament he exacted tonnage and poundage, demanded a loan of £100,000 from the city of London, which, on being refused, he changed for a forced loan equal in amount to five subsidies, about £350,000. Refusal in this case was visited with punishment, gentlemen being sent to prison and ordinary men enlisted as soldiers. Other means of raising money were resorted to also, one being the levying of shipmoney upon all the counties, a tax hitherto only laid upon the maritime counties and that in time of war merely. Strong was the resentment and loud the discontent of the nation at these proceedings.

But while some were protesting, the Court section of the clergy took sides with the King and began to exalt the royal prerogative. Dr. Sibthorpe of Burton Latimer, in his assize sermon at Northampton, maintained that the King possessed legislative power and that all resistance to the royal will was actually sinful. Dr. Mainwaring also, in a sermon preached before the King himself, denied that the consent of Parliament was necessary to taxation. For this offence the Lords imprisoned and deprived him, but the King at once pardoned him and gave him the rectory of Stanford Rivers. This was in 1628, and on January 20, 1629, Parliament assembled, the third of the reign, meeting the King in no friendly mood.

When business began other matters besides taxation came up for debate. In a Declaration the previous November, the King had ratified and confirmed the Articles as containing the true doctrine of the Church of England, and by way of putting an end to the curious and unhappy differences so long prevailing in the Church, enjoined all preachers to keep to them and put all curious search aside. Sir John Eliot pointed out that this enjoining of silence was one-sided, for while limiting

the Puritan it gave full freedom to the Anglo-Catholic.
On January 26, a Committee on Religion was formed
to consider the subject of religious grievances, which
formulated a series of resolutions to be brought before
the House. They pointed to the threatening dangers
from the growth of Popery, and to the fact that Anglo-
Catholicism, which they called the Arminian faction, was
separating them from the Reformed Churches abroad
and bringing divisions at home. They drew attention to
the introduction of new ceremonies in worship, to the
erection of altars in place of communion tables; to the
bringing men to question and trouble for not standing
up at the *Gloria Patri*; to the publishing of books and the
preaching of sermons contrary to the orthodox doctrine,
while books and sermons from the other side were
rigidly suppressed. They further pleaded that bishoprics
and other preferments should not be conferred upon
those who practiced superstitious ceremonies, but upon
learned, pious and orthodox men; that non-residence
of clergy be put a stop to, and means be provided for
maintaining a godly, able minister in every parish. The
King took alarm at these resolutions and ordered an
adjournment of the House, and again, on the 2nd of
March, the Speaker declared the King's pleasure that
it should be adjourned until the 10th. He was met with
cries of "No!" and Eliot rose to speak. The Speaker
said he had an absolute command from the King to

leave the chair if any one spoke; he was, however, held down in the chair by main force; Eliot asserted the right of the House to adjourn itself; the doors were locked and three resolutions were put to the vote and carried by acclamation. These were: (1) That whosoever shall bring in innovations in religion, or opinions disagreeing from the true and orthodox Church should be reputed a capital enemy to this kingdom and the commonwealth; (2) Whosoever should counsel or advise the levying of taxes and subsidies not being granted by Parliament should be reputed an innovator in the government and a capital enemy to the State; and (3) That any merchant or person voluntarily paying such taxes and subsidies not being granted by Parliament should be reputed a betrayer of the liberties of England and an enemy to the same. Nine members of the House of Commons were imprisoned for their part in these proceedings; Parliament was dissolved and then for eleven years England was governed without any Parliament at all. The significant fact about that eventful day in Parliament was that in the three resolutions passed, there was a union of religious discontent and political discontent. Elizabeth's policy had created a religious opposition, and the policy of James and Charles had created a political opposition; and by the three resolutions of March 2, 1629, these two causes had become one, and out of this union came the Long Parliament of 1640, and the Civil War, with the consequent downfall of Church and King.

During the long years when England was under the personal government of Charles I, the Church continued to pursue the course dictated to it by Archbishop Laud. As a man after the King's own heart he had received preferment after preferment, rising rapidly to power till he had attained to the highest position in the Church, and had become the King's most trusted ecclesiastical adviser. A martinet in all matters of form and ceremony, and unwearied at work, his influence was felt at every point. Nothing was too great for him to aim at, nothing too minute for him to care for. He had untiring perseverance, the instinct of order and a passion for detail. He was just as earnest and persistent in getting rails erected round the communion table of the parish church and com-pelling the people to kneel there, as he was in trying to revolutionize the religion of the whole realm of Scotland by bringing it over from Presbyterianism to Episcopacy.

Laud's policy was the one prominent and preeminent fact in the history of the Church of England during the years between 1629 and 1640. Among the clergy he prohibited the least manifestation of nonconformity or individuality. They were no longer to be permitted to omit this or that prayer at pleasure, to stand when they were bidden to kneel, or to kneel when they were bidden to stand. So far as the laity were concerned they were to be treated as children and made to subject their own individuality to that of their spiritual pastors and masters; were forbidden to leave their own parish church, to attend even episcopal services elsewhere. In parish after parish Puritan ministers were compelled, contrary to the established custom, to set the communion table altar-wise, to place altar rails, and require the people to come from their seats and receive the sacrament kneeling.

As the records of the time show, this last requirement raised a burning question as between Puritan and Anglo-Catholic. Was the communion table a table or an altar? Should it be placed in the body of the church or chancel or set altar-wise at the east end? In Elizabeth's time a compromise had been come to which was substantially adopted in the Canons of 1604 to the effect that the table should stand in the church where the altar stood before the Reformation, except at the celebration of the Communion, when it was to be brought out and placed where the communicants could most conveniently see and hear the minister. And in nearly all the parish churches it kept its place in the middle of the church or chancel, and any attempt to remove it was resented by the parishioners as a step towards popery. In St. Gregory's Church, St. Paul's, the dean and chapter had placed the table in the east end setting rails before it, whereupon five parishioners appealed to the Court of Arches against this proceeding. The King himself then appeared on the scene, summoned the five before the Privy Council and sharply

OLIVER CROMWELL

told them that the placing of the communion table was no business of theirs. This was in 1633, and in 1635, Archbishop Laud gave orders that the table should in all churches be moved to the east end and be railed in. This order was met by stout resistance. The churchwardens of Beckington were excommunicated for refusing to obey, and thrown into prison. The opposition was especially strong in the dioceses of Lincoln and Norwich. In spite of resistance, however, in parish after parish Laud carried his way, but with disastrous results to the best interests of the Church.

In 1634 the archbishop revived the long disused claim to Metropolitical Visitation, sending his vicar-general to report upon the ecclesiastical condition of the province of Canterbury. This was Sir Nathaniel Brent, who began with the diocese of Lincoln and worked his way southwards. He unearthed strange doings and met with curious experiences. He also carried out some much-needed reforms; for he had to report that alehouses, hounds and swine were kept in churchyards; that copes and vestments had been embezzled; that clandestine marriages were celebrated by the clergy, and that both clergy and laity were much given to drunkenness. His chief attentions, however, were bestowed upon the Puritan portion of the clergy. He reports "at Huntingdon divers ministers in that division were suspected of Puritanisme"; and of Bedford, which he reached on the

26th of August, he says, "Mr Peter Bulkeley, rector of Odell, suspected for Puritanisme was suspended for non-appearance. He came to me at Aylesburie, where he confessed he never used the surplisse or the cross in baptisme. He is to appear in the High Commission Court the first court day in November, if he reform not before." Peter Bulkeley, who was of resolute Puritan stock—his sister also being the mother of Oliver St. John, who was afterwards Cromwell's Lord Chief Justice—resolved to leave the country rather than conform. The Pilgrim Fathers, who had sailed from Leyden and founded the old Plymouth Colony in New England in 1620, were followed ten years later by other Englishmen of Puritan faith, who founded the towns round Massachusetts Bay and along the Connecticut River, exercising a powerful influence upon the future of American religious life. There were among them laymen possessed of wealth and social position, and many ministers who had occupied influential positions in the Church. Between 1629 and 1640 about ninety university men, three-fourths of them from Cambridge, had emigrated. Of these Cambridge men, while nine were of Trinity and nine from St. John's, no fewer than twenty-two were of Emmanuel College, the Puritan foundation of Sir Walter Mildmay. In this list of twenty-two are found the great names of John Cotton, Thomas Hooker, R Saltonstall, Thomas Shepard and John Harvard. It has been estimated upon what seem fairly reliable data that as the result of Laud's administration some 4000 Puritan families, or an aggregate of over 20,000 persons went over to New England. With the exception of the Pilgrim Fathers, who sailed in the *Mayflower* in 1620, these were not Separatists. Francis Higginson, vicar of one of the five parishes of Leicester, who sailed with the first party in 1629, may be taken as representative of all the rest. As the ship was off the Land's End, he and his companions stood on deck to take the last farewell look of the land they were leaving and which they loved so well. Standing there and looking eastward till the coastline faded out of sight, he said: "We will not say as the Separatists were wont to say at their leaving of England, "Farewell, Babylon, farewell, Rome," but we will say, "Farewell, dear England, farewell, the Church of God in England, and all the Christian friends there." We do not go to New England as Separatists from the Church of England, though we cannot but separate from the corruptions in it."

CHAPTER VI

PURITANISM *in its* TRIUMPH *and* DOWNFALL

Through the series of years during which Charles I was governing England without Parliament, and Laud was harassing both clergy and laity by his highhanded ways, the forces of opposition were steadily gaining strength against them both. On the constitutional question the significant words of Sir John Eliot, spoken when the struggle began, had not been forgotten, when he said—"Upon this dispute not alone our goods and lands are engaged, but all that we call ours. Those rights, those privileges which made our fathers free men are in question." On the religious question also there was deepening determination to resist ecclesiastical oppression, and Puritanism was steadily growing in numbers and influence. These two forces were now making common cause with each other against the day of reckoning. That day came when on the 3rd of November, 1640, that Long Parliament assembled which was to change so much before it reached its end. The King was urgent for a money grant to relieve him of the consequences of his Scottish war, but the Commons being in no conciliatory mood demanded redress of grievances before voting supply. And as in their view the religious grievance took precedence of the constitutional, they concentrated their attack upon the Canons recently passed in Convocation. A Committee of twenty-four was appointed to prepare a Declaration on the State of the Kingdom, the Book of Canons being referred to the Grand Committee for Religion.

Meantime an ominous petition against Episcopacy was presented to the House by citizens of London which was signed by 15,000 persons, its delivery in Westminster Hall being attended by no fewer than 1500 gentlemen of the city. This document, known as the Root-and-Branch petition is to be distinguished from the Root-and-Branch *Bill* of the following May. It covered a wide range of ecclesiastical grievances. Among the evils complained of was the silencing of so many faithful, diligent and powerful ministers because they could not in conscience submit to the needless devices of the bishops; and also the great increase of idle, lewd, dissolute and ignorant ministers. The petitioners also protested against the great and growing conformity of the Church of England to the Church of Rome in vestures, postures, ceremonies and administrations. Entering into detail they objected to the bowing towards the altar, and the setting of images, crucifixes and conceits over it or tapers upon it; they disliked and protested against the christening and consecrating of buildings, fonts, tables, pulpits, chalices and churchyards, thereby putting holiness upon things inanimate. Finally, besides other grievances, they complained of inquisitorial proceedings extending even to men's thoughts; the apprehending and detaining men by pursuivants; the frequent suspending and depriving of ministers; the fining and imprisonment of all sorts of people; and other outrages contrary to the laws of the realm and the subjects' liberties. This petition from London was followed by others from the counties of Kent, Essex and Suffolk, that from Kent having 2500 names attached.

A month later there followed the document known as the "Ministers' Petition and Remonstrance," setting forth their grievances from their own point of view. They denied that diocesan bishops are a divine institution and objected to their assuming sole power of ordination and jurisdiction; they objected also to the delegation of the bishops' power to unmeet persons; to the imposing of the oath of canonical obedience and the enforcing of subscription; to the demanding of exorbitant fees on institution to a living; and, finally, they objected to the judicial power of the bishops in Parliament, in the Star Chamber, in the Commissions of the Peace and at the Council Table. These petitions were followed by others, from no fewer than eleven counties, for the abolition of Episcopacy, that from Suffolk having as many as 4400 names attached, and that from Norfolk 2000. These various petitions were all referred to the Committee of twenty-four, out of which to prepare heads for the consideration of the House.

The following May the Houses passed a Bill depriving the King of the power to dissolve Parliament without its own consent, and on the 27th of the same month, Sir E. Bering, the member for Kent, moved the first reading of the Root-and-Branch Bill entitled "An Act for the utter abolishing and taking away of all archbishops, bishops, their chancellors, commissaries, deans, deans and chapters, archdeacons, prebendaries, chanters arid canons and all other their under officers." In doing this he spoke regretfully of the necessity he felt to be laid upon him. "I never was for ruin," he said, "so long as I could hope any hope of reforming. My hopes that way are now almost withered. When this Bill is perfected I shall give a sad 'Aye' to it." The Bill was read a second time the same day by a majority of 139 to 108 and referred to a Committee of the whole House. Here, after dealing with the preamble, they proceeded to the consideration of the clause for abolishing the offices of archbishops, bishops and the rest of the superior clergy; and then, on June 15, with the question of deans and chapters, recording their decision that these officers be taken out of the Church and their lands appropriated to the advancement of learning and piety. It was further decided that the Ecclesiastical Courts should cease from and after the 1st of August; and that to replace the government thus superseded, the whole jurisdiction should be in the hands of nine chief commissioners who should appoint five ministers in every county for purposes of ordination.

At this point the Bill rested in Committee, for grave matters were felt to be impending, the King having announced his intention to visit Scotland, from which serious questions would be likely to arise. Parliament, having resumed, proceeded to deal with Laud's innovations. Commissions were appointed to visit the various counties for the defacing, demolishing and quite taking away of all images, altars, or tables turned altar-wise, crucifixes, superstitious pictures, ornaments and relics of idolatry out of all churches and chapels. These orders passed, the House adjourned to October 20.

Parliament, on reassembling, addressed itself first of all to what is known as the Grand Remonstrance, which was practically a long indictment of the King's conduct ever since his accession, to which he only replied by speaking disdainfully of their proposed ecclesiastical reforms. This he followed up by the attempted Arrest of the Five Members who had taken a leading part in formulating the Remonstrance. Though he was baffled in this, it practically brought on a crisis from which he felt there could be no escape but by an appeal to arms. On the 22nd of August, therefore, Charles I set up the royal standard on Nottingham Hill, and called upon all loyal subjects to come to his aid against a rebellious Parliament. Once more, therefore, the nation was plunged into Civil War, the allegiance of the people being challenged, not as in the Wars of the Roses, by rival Houses, but claimed by the rival authorities of King and Parliament. It was not a Social War, but one of those conflicts of ideas that recur at intervals in the course of history, and always with tragic issue. For in a conflict of ideas the noblest minds, because of their very nobility are resolutely averse to compromise, and cannot reconcile themselves to defeat. This war was for sovereign right on the part of the people as well as on that of the King. Colonel Hutchinson said that it was on the question of civil right he joined with the Parliament, and though he was satisfied the endeavors of their opponents tended to subvert the protestant religion, "he did not think that so clear a ground for the war as the defence of English liberties." Cromwell also speaking on the subject twelve years after the war broke out, said distinctly that "Religion was not the thing at first contested for, but God brought it to that issue at last, and at last it proved to be that which was most dear to us." And certainly, as we follow the course of events, it becomes clear that it was not Presbyterianism that brought on the war, but the war that brought in Presbyterianism. This system became organized in England in the seventeenth century, not as a matter of national preference, but of military necessity. For by the end of 1643 the outlook for the parliamentary party, so far as the war was concerned, was most depressing. The west, with few exceptions, had declared for the King, so had the north with the exception of Hull and Lancashire, and while Parliament had gained strength in the eastern counties, it held the midlands only with difficulty.

In anxious condition the Puritans turned to their brethren in Scotland, and in November, 1643, the Scottish Parliament agreed to send 21,000 men to their assistance, but only on the understanding that the Solemn League and Covenant should be accepted in England as it had been in Scotland, and so pledge the two nations to unite for the reformation of religion according to the Word of God and the example of the best Reformed Churches. There were many in England who were willing to modify or even set aside Episcopacy, but there were many also who favored congregational independence, which would be as rigorously repressed under the Scottish system as it had been under the bishops; and there were few who were willing to introduce into England the inquisitorial jurisdiction exercised by the Church courts in Scotland. The necessity, however, was urgent; military help must be had and it could only be had on the terms offered. When it had passed both Houses, the Commons and the Assembly of Divines swore to the Solemn League and Covenant on September 25; and somewhat later the few Peers who still lingered at Westminster swore to it also. The following February it was universally imposed upon all Englishmen over eighteen years of age, the names of those refusing to be formally certified.

The General Assembly in Edinburgh having laid it down that there could be no hope of unity in religion till there be one form of ecclesiastical government, a parliamentary ordinance was passed on August 19, 1645, for the setting up of Presbyterian government as the national form of religion. The parish churches of London, one hundred and thirty-seven in number, were to be arranged in twelve classes, the Chapel of the Rolls, the two Serjeants' Inns, and the four Inns of Court together making up the thirteenth. For the country at large county committees were to map out classical districts, the several classes as approved by Parliament to have power to constitute congregational elderships. These elderships corresponding to the Kirk session of the Scottish Church were to meet once a week, the classes corresponding to the presbytery once a month, the provincial synod twice a year, and the National Assembly to meet in session as summoned by Parliament and not otherwise. By a second parliamentary ordinance dated March 14, 1646, it was commanded that a choice of elders be made forthwith throughout the kingdom of England and dominion of Wales, in their respective churches and chapels. Thus, so far as legislation was concerned, but no further, the new presbyterian system was ready to become an actual reality in the national life.

The system of Church government thus made absolute by ordinance of Parliament was sufficiently rigid. Its basis was, of course, parochial. Every parishioner living within a given area was required to take his place in the parochial organization and submit to the parochial authorities. Every parish congregation was to choose its representative to sit in the Provincial or National Assembly, and no ecclesiastical community except that of the parish was to be allowed to exist. This was altogether too narrow for some who had been fighting for freedom as against King and prelate; and Oliver Cromwell obtained an Order from the House that an endeavor should be made to find some way how far "tender consciences who cannot in all things submit to the common rule which shall be established, may be borne with according to the Word and as may stand with the public peace." Baillie, one of the Scottish commissioners, writes: "This order presentlie gave us the alarm. We saw it was a toleration of the Independents by Act of Parliament before the Presbytery was established." However, when the matter came up again, on report of committee, Cromwell's proposal to consider tender consciences was negatived without division. This was on the 6th of January, 1645, and on the 13th the House gave its assent to the ordinary presbyterian system by a resolution that parochial congregations should be combined in groups under presbyteries.

The independents still protested on behalf of a freer system, and Jeremiah Burroughs, one of their number, gave voice to their feeling in a sermon preached before the Lords in Westminster Abbey. It saddened his heart, he said, that those who not long since were crying to heaven for deliverance should now rise up to oppose a forbearance of their brethren who, together with them, love Jesus Christ, and agree with them in the substance of worship and the doctrinal part of religion. Votes in Parliament may have their value, but the power that rightly influences conscience is light from the Word. "To use force upon people," he went on to say, "before they have means to teach them is to seek to beat the nail of authority without making way by the wimble of instruction. If you have to deal with rotten or sappy wood the hammer only may make the nail enter presently, but if you meet with sound wood, with heart of oak, though the hammer and hand that strike be strong, yet the nail will hardly go in. It will turn crooked or break…. Consider you have to deal with English consciences; there is no country so famous for firm strong oaks as England. You will find English consciences to be so."

These words were clear and strong, and they were backed up immediately by irresistible facts. For on the 15th of June, 1646, the battle of Naseby was fought and won by the independents, by Cromwell and the army of the New Model—the army which he had reorganized by filling its ranks with men of godly principles and earnest purpose. And when they had won that decisive victory, he maintained on their behalf that they were entitled to the fruits of victory in the shape of religious freedom. Writing to the Speaker of the House of Commons from the field of battle, to announce the great news of the day, Cromwell said: "Honest men served you faithfully in this action. Sir, they are trusty; I beseech you in the name of God not to discourage them. He that ventures his life for the liberty of his country, I wish he trust God for the liberty of his conscience, and you for the liberty he fights for."

But the time of larger religious freedom was not yet. The battle of Naseby was fought on the 15th of June, 1646, and on the 22nd of May, 1647, a London crowd was gathered round a fire kindled in front of the Royal Exchange, to see the sheriffs of London and Middlesex

CHARLES I

burn a petition which had been circulated in the city for signature, and had given great offence to Parliament. It was a petition in favor of religious freedom, desiring that no man might be punished or persecuted as heretical, by judges that are not infallible, for preaching or publishing his opinions in a peaceable way. For, upon pretence of suppressing errors, sects and schisms, the most necessary truths and sincere professions thereof may be suppressed. This petition being brought to the notice of the House of Commons was by resolution ordered to be burnt, and some of those who had signed it were sent to gaol. There was clearly no hope of larger liberty from Parliament, for there the men who were opposed to religious toleration were steadily gaining the upper hand. "To let men serve God according to the persuasion of their own consciences," wrote a presbyterian divine, "was to cast out one devil that seven worse might enter." "We detest and abhor the much endeavoured toleration," declared a meeting of the London ministers. On the 2nd of September, 1646, an ordinance for the suppression of blasphemy and heresy was introduced into the House of Commons which actually went the length of proposing that any denial of the doctrines of the Trinity and the Incarnation should be punished by death, whilst denial of other less important doctrines such as those relating to presbyterian government and Infant Baptism should be punished with imprisonment for life.

This atrocious ordinance was actually read twice in the House of Commons without a division and sent before a committee of the whole House, and the Journals of the House remain to testify the fact [C. J. IV. 659]. The Lords also drew up an ordinance forbidding all who were not ordained ministers "to preach or expound the Scriptures in any church or chapel, or in any other place." On the 31st of December, 1646, this ordinance was sent down to the Commons. The independents, knowing there was no hope of their getting the measure rejected, sought merely to amend it, so far at least as to allow laymen to expound the Scriptures. Long and stormy was the debate which followed and when the division came on, Cromwell himself acting as one of the tellers, he and his party were defeated by 105 to 57. A further motion to restrict the prohibition to places "appointed for public worship," was defeated without a division.

It is at this point in the history we come upon the line of division between the presbyterians and the independents. The Scots army finding that the King never really meant to accept presbyterianism prepared to leave the country. By the 11th of February every garrison had been delivered up, every Scottish soldier had recrossed the Tweed, and the King's person had been left in charge of the Parliamentary Commissioners and a guard of cavalry at Holmby House. Still, before his arrival there, a number of presbyterian peers had agreed with him to accept certain concessions he was prepared to make as the basis of an agreement, upon the completion of which Charles was to be restored to Crown and Kingdom. It was the beginning of an alliance between the presbyterians and the royalists which thirteen years later was to bring about the Restoration of the Monarchy and the Church. It was also the widening of the divergence between presbyterian and independent, for if the concessions proposed were admitted, it would mean the surrender of everything for which the independents had been contending since the war began. But now, the army being disbanded, they were powerless to resist. For all the general officers of the "New Model," except Fairfax, were to be dismissed; and no Member of Parliament could hold a commission in the new army, or any officer be employed, who did not conform to the presbyterian discipline. But while great changes were made, and the army was no longer on a war footing, 4000 of the soldiers of the "New Model" were retained in England, having their quarters at Saffron Walden. At this juncture these became restive and defiant, and when Cornet Joyce, with 500 mounted troopers, rode over to Holmby House and took possession of the King's person, the situation was vitally changed.

What happened after this can only be briefly summarized. The execution of the King in 1649 was followed by a declaration of Parliament that "England shall henceforth be governed as a Common-wealth or Free State, by a supreme authority of this nation, the representatives of the people in Parliament." But the Parliament thus taking to itself supreme power had really ceased to be representative of the national will. By the expulsion of royalist members during the war and of presbyterians in 1648 it had, as Cromwell said, been "winnowed and sifted and brought to a handfull." When first elected in 1640 it consisted of 490 members; in January, 1649, there were not more than ninety. Four counties, Lancashire being one of them, had no representatives at all; Wales had only three and London one. Yet, though it was thus only a mere remnant of its former self, this Parliament continued to sit on, and sat all the year round; and moreover, by an Act passed in 1641, it could not be adjourned, prorogued or dissolved except by its own consent. In 1653 it was discussing a Bill providing for its own continuance, and for still retaining in its own hands both legislative and executive power, when Cromwell hurried down to the House, and by an act of revolutionary violence dismissed this which has been described as once the most powerful Parliament ever known in England.

But now the urgent question was what should take its place. After much discussion, and not a little disagreement, Cromwell and the council of the army decided to call a Parliament of Puritan notables, the congregational churches of the various counties being invited to send up the names of persons fit to be members, from which a selection might be made. Eventually the list included 160 persons. There was no pretence of election, and the assembly thus formed came to be known as the Little Parliament of 1653, and sometimes, by way of ridicule, as Barebone's Parliament, from the name of one of its members. But though thus made the butt of ridicule on the part of cavaliers, it contained not a few distinguished and capable men and did not a little useful work. It abolished the Court of Chancery, where 23,000 cases of from five to thirty years' standing were lying undetermined. It established civil marriages and provided for the registration of births, marriages and burials; and a committee was also appointed to codify the law. But reforms, as these men found full soon, create enemies, and though they were entitled to sit till 1654, by the end of 1653 they abdicated their places and surrendered their powers into the hands of Cromwell as Protector of the Commonwealth.

After being solemnly installed on December 16, 1653, according to the "Instrument of Government" he and his council were empowered to issue ordinances having the force of law "until order shall be taken in Parliament concerning them," the first triennial Parliament to meet in September, 1654. Cromwell took full advantage of this his opportunity, and the nine months when he was thus practically absolute have been described as the really creative period of his government. He issued eighty-two ordinances, nearly all of which were confirmed in 1656 by his second Parliament. Those of them most characteristic of his domestic policy are the three divisions bearing upon the reform of the law, the reformation of manners and the reorganization of the National Church. His purpose was, as he said, to make the laws of man "conformable to the just and righteous laws of God." Some English laws, he told Parliament, were "wicked and abominable laws," and he protested against hanging a man for six and eightpence; "to see men lose their lives for petty matters is a thing God will reckon."

In the reformation of manners Parliament went faster than they carried public opinion with them; and Cromwell's major-generals by peremptory harshness made Puritan legislation to be spoken of as Puritan tyranny. The observance of the Sabbath, for example, was enforced not merely to the extent of closing shops and stoppage of manufacture, but so far as to put an end to all travelling on that day except in cases of necessity attested by certificate from a justice of the peace; and persons "vainly and profanely walking on the day aforesaid" were to be punished. These major-generals, while looking to the maintenance of order, were to control the local authorities, put down horse-races, bear-baitings and cockfights, to expel vagrants, close unnecessary alehouses, cause drunkenness to be duly punished, and even report to the council all justices who were negligent in discharging the duties of their office. It is on record that alehouses were closed by the hundred; and beggars, idlers and debauched persons were arrested in such numbers that the authorities were at a loss where to imprison them, and called for wholesale transportation. Many things they did which were in the interest of morality and public order, but, unfortunately, were too often done in a way to create deep discontent and rouse a storm of opposition.

Still it must not be forgotten that, while seeking to reform the morals of the nation by process of law, Cromwell really laid more stress on the influence of education and religion. When making an educational grant for Scotland he declared that it was "a duty not only to have the Gospel set up, but schools for children erected and maintained therefor." Milton, too, advocated the foundation of schools in all parts of the nation; and Harrington in his *Oceana* (1656) asserted that the formation of future citizens by means of a system of free schools was one of the chief duties of a republic. In 1651 Cromwell strongly urged the endowment in the north of a school or college for all the sciences and literature out of the property of the dean and chapter of Durham.

It need not be said that he was also as solicitous about the religion of the nation as for the education of its citizens. These were not for him two questions but only two sides of one question, that of the elevation of the people. Dealing with this it was found necessary to reorganize the system of the National Church. For though the presbyterian discipline had been established by Parliament, the ecclesiastical condition was far from working smoothly. It was found out then, not for the first time or the last, that it is one thing to create a constitution by Parliament and quite another to make it a vital part of the nation's life. The minutes of the provincial assemblies make it only too clear that a form of church government, accepted under constraint and unwillingly, went heavily on its way. There was opposition and, what was perhaps worse, there was indifference on the part of a large body of the laity. In January, 1648, the London synod reported that four out of the twelve classes appointed by Parliament had not yet been formed and therefore had sent no dele-gates. And even four years later, in 1652, in an appeal made by the provincial assembly fears were expressed of "the utter dissolution of presbyterian government." There was greater difficulty still with the parochial elderships. It was reported from St. Matthew's, Friday Street, that "the minister hath endeavoured to get elders chosen, but cannot move his parishioners to it"; and from St. Peter's, Paul's Wharf, also, "that the people cannot be induced to choose elders, nor to have a minister that may act with the Government." In many other places also through the country there were churches which declined to elect elders and set up discipline. In Lancashire the presbyterian system obtained more widely than elsewhere, yet even there its efficient working was in many places hampered either by indifference or open hostility. Adam Martindale tells us that in his own parish of Gorton the system could not be worked because some were against ruling elders as unscriptural and strangers in antiquity, while several were downright for the congregational way, and yet others did not like to be under the power of ruling elders who might have been chosen at some place ten miles away from them.

The case being so, it was no easy task to which Cromwell put his hand when in 1654 he and his council proceeded to reorganize the National Church system. Men like Milton and Sir Harry Vane were opposed to a State Church altogether. The magistrates, Milton contended, had no coercive power at all in matters of religion. It was not his business "to settle religion," to use the current phrase, "by appointing either what we shall believe in divine things or practice in religion." On the other hand, the framers of the "Instrument of Government" were invincibly opposed to the voluntary system. All therefore that Cromwell and his council could do in the way of ecclesiastical organization was to determine in what way the ministers of the National Church should be appointed or dismissed, how far restrained in their teaching, and from what sources they should be paid. The State, then, had nothing to say as to forms of ordination, or even whether there was to be ordination at all. All that it concerned itself with when a minister appeared before them was, as to whether he had a right to maintenance as secured to ministers under certain conditions laid down by law. This was to be determined by a body of commissioners, known as Triers, consisting of ministers and laymen who might content themselves with requiring the certificate of three persons testifying to the holy and good conversation of the person to be admitted to the benefice. The right of the patron to present to the benefice remained intact and unchallenged. All that the Triers could do was to see that he did not present an unfit person. In the State Church system thus reconstructed in 1654 there was no one recognized form of ecclesiastical organization, and therefore no mention made by name either of episcopacy, presbyterianism or independency. There were no Church courts, no Church assemblies, no Church laws or ordinances. Nothing was said about rites and ceremonies, nothing even about sacraments. The mode of administering the Lord's Supper and baptism was left an open question to be determined by each congregation for itself. It was further provided that if there were churches that preferred to worship outside the national system altogether they were at liberty to do so. The Articles of Government declared that such persons "shall not be restrained, but shall be protected in the profession of the faith and exercise of their religion, so as they abuse not their liberty to the civil injury of others, and to the actual disturbance of the public peace on their part." Of course it must be admitted that the liberty was "not to extend to popery or prelacy." But on this point, Dr. Rawson Gardiner, an ideally fair-minded historian, has this to say: "With the exception of the condemnation of the use of the Common Prayer, the scheme was in the highest sense broad and generous; and it is well to remember that those who strove to reserve the use of the Common Prayer were a political as well as an ecclesiastical party, and that the weight and activity of that party, except so far as it appealed to the indifferent in religion, were out of all proportion to its numbers."

In his National Church settlement Cromwell seems honestly to have aimed at bringing about a real union of tolerance and comprehension. How far his experiment might have succeeded had longer time been granted to it can only be left to conjecture. But the requisite conditions depended on the continuance of his own life. He was the one strong man in the nation, the only one able to control and combine the conflicting elements of the time, and he was not suffered to continue. Prodigal of his great soul, he had, in the high places of the war and in the strenuous work of government, lavishly spent his vital force till, old before his time, he passed away on the 3rd of September, 1658.

When Cromwell fell the rule of the Puritan fell with him. The scepter of sovereignty having passed to feebler hands, conflicting forces, both religious and political, which had been held in check, now rose in tumult, and confusion reigned supreme. But while hostility to Puritanism on the part of some of the people was one of the forces which brought about the downfall of the Commonwealth, it was not the only one, nor the one that was strongest. Sir Henry Vane attacked the validity of Richard Cromwell's title, and made alliance with the army against him, yet there was no more fervent Puritan than Sir Henry Vane. The presbyterians, again, formed the great body of the Puritan party; they far outnumbered the independents, and it was by their action, and theirs alone, that the Solemn League and Covenant was enforced upon the English people; yet the restoration of the monarchy was mainly brought about by the presbyterians. They supposed that Charles II meant what he said when in his declaration from Breda he promised that liberty should be secured to tender consciences; and, with a credulity at which one can only wonder, they believed in 1659 as they had believed in 1649 that they could secure his consent to the national establishment of the presbyterian system of Church government. They had always been adherents of monarchy, and the Convention Parliament which succeeded the Long Parliament, and by which the King was restored, was half of it presbyterian.

It was not only, nor mainly, dislike of Puritanism that brought about the counter-revolution of 1660. There was the weariness resulting from incessant change and uncertainty; there was the deep-seated love of monarchical government in the heart of the English people; there was the revulsion of feeling brought about by the beheading of King Charles I, for it may be truly said that the execution of the King brought back the King, it made men forget his misdeeds and invested him with the sanctity of a martyr—these and other forces of political sort combined together to bring down the commonwealth. When that came down, Puritanism, which had gone out of power when the army was disbanded, came down with it. So far as its influence in the State was concerned, an influence which at one time had been paramount, its fall was as sudden, complete and overwhelming as its triumph had been rapid and surprising. When it held the reins of government, it made the rulers of Europe not only to respect England but to fear her. And then the wheel went full cycle round. Those of its leaders who escaped death, exile and imprisonment had to undergo proscription, and fell into obscurity. Men who had been pillars of the State, victorious in war, and conspicuous in the eyes of the civilized world were deprived of the most elementary rights of citizenship. Triumphant Puritans became helpless and persecuted noncomformists. Puritanism passed through more than a quarter of a century of cruel oppression and suffering, but there is often a soul of good in things evil, and that time of relentless persecution created sacred traditions which have borne fruit in consecrated lives. Puritanism, rightly looked at, is not a thing of one time but for all time. It stands for the supremacy of the will of heaven against the passions and clamors of earth. Its defect has too often been that it gave too narrow an interpretation of what really is the will of heaven. The principles at the heart of it—obedience and righteousness—are the binding forces without which society would go to pieces; but while recognizing the value of these it failed, at least many of its followers failed, to recognize also the value of the more graceful and genial elements of human life, without which its glory and blessedness are not complete.

But while thus much may be conceded, it must at the same time be contended that the men of the Commonwealth were by no means the harsh and narrow-minded fanatics, looking grimly upon all fair and pleasant things in life, which cavalier writers have sought to make them appear. Cromwell certainly condemned no innocent pleasures. He himself hunted, hawked and played the games of the time as did the royalist country gentlemen who were his neighbors, and had as real a love for a fine horse as they. One of his contemporaries tells us that he was "a great lover of music and entertained the most skilful in that science in his pay and family," and that when he gave a banquet to foreign ambassadors "rare music both of instruments and voices" was one of the features of the entertainment. To his credit, too, in matters of art it must be remembered that he saved the cartoons of Raphael and the "Triumph" of Mantegna for the nation, whereas in later years Charles II tried to sell them to the King of France. Milton, again, his Latin secretary, no man can call a narrow-minded fanatic, but rather a man of loftiest genius whose "soul was like a star and dwelt apart," a poet having a voice "whose sound was like the sea: pure as the naked heavens, majestic, free." And turning from Cromwell and Milton, we may recall the picture of Colonel Hutchinson, the governor of Nottingham Castle, as given to us by his Puritan wife. While "his faith being established in the truth he was full of love to God and all His saints," not less than any of his royalist neighbors was he graced with the ordinary accomplishments of life, "had skill in fencing such as became a gentleman, great love of music, playing masterly on the viol, and had great judgement in paintings, gravings, sculpture, and all liberal arts, and had many curiosities in all kinds."

It is admitted that the Puritans were averse to dramatic representations and hostile to the stage. The reason for this Kingsley has given us. He has shown that, with the exception of Shakespeare, it was the custom of the comedies of the seventeenth century to introduce adultery as a subject for laughter, and often as the staple of the whole plot, the seducer being let pass as a "handsome gentleman" and the injured husband made the object of every kind of scorn and ridicule. And he thinks that most people nowadays will surely "agree with the Puritans that adultery is not a subject for comedy. It may be for tragedy, but for comedy, never."

To this question of Puritanism, then, as to so many others, there are two sides, one of serious estimate, and another of burlesque and travesty. And time tries both. Puritan institutions in the seventeenth century fell with Cromwell, but Puritan ideas did not fall with the institutions in which they had been embodied. They had done a great and permanent work in the sacred cause of liberty. The Puritans arrested the growth of absolute government in England, a growth which had made rapid advance under the personal government of the Tudors and was fatally proceeding under the Stuart kings who succeeded them. And what made it the more dangerous was that it had succeeded among the other nations of Europe. As we have already seen, absolute monarchies had everywhere else risen on the ruins of national liberties, so that a man could rise in Parliament in 1625 and declare that the English were the last people in Christendom that maintained their rights. How long might they be able to say they were doing so? It was the turning-point of national destiny, and it was Puritanism that came to the rescue. The situation demanded that religious enthusiasm should go hand in hand with the love of liberty, to resist the encroachments of the Prince. It has been truly said that Puritan zeal turned the scale in the conflict between divine right and parliamentary authority. So that if Puritanism fell, it fell in the hour of victory. The Stuart kings came back, but there did not come back with them the Star Chamber, or the Court of high Commission, or ship-money or forced loans and benevolences. The battle of constitutional liberty had been fought and won.

APPENDIX A

OLIVER CROMWELL: LORD PROTECTOR *of* ENGLAND, SCOTLAND, *and* IRELAND

by Joe Morecraft, III

It was said of Oliver Cromwell that he "in the world of action was what Shakespeare was in the world of art, the greatest and most powerful Englishman of all time."[1] Theodore Roosevelt said of him that he was "the greatest Englishman of the Seventeenth Century" and had in fact "headed a movement that produced the English-speaking world as we at present know it."[2] Thomas Carlyle said, with some hyperbole, that Cromwell was "the last glimpse of the God-like vanishing from England."[3] And Merle D'Aubigne, the great Reformed historian, said that Oliver Cromwell was the greatest Christian since Martin Luther and John Calvin. He also said that "rarely has there appeared in the world a heart that beat so strongly for everlasting truth."[4]

Why did these scholars, along with many others, give such high praise for this man, when most people today think of him as a hypocrite and a dictator? This brief sketch of Cromwell's life will seek to answer this.

THE HISTORICAL CONTEXT OF CROMWELL'S BIRTH

By the time of Cromwell's birth on August 25, 1599, the Protestant Reformation was in full force in Europe and the British Isles. Queen Elizabeth was in the last years of her long reign (1558-1603). She had suppressed Puritanism, but not as severely as her predecessor and half-sister, Mary Tudor, better known as "Bloody Mary."

Europe was in turmoil. In about half a century, one generation of Europeans had seen "the Peasants' War, the Sack of Rome, the split of Northern and Southern Germany, divisions among the Cantons of Switzerland, the break of England from the Vatican, and more wars, battles, executions, massacres, arguments and new books, atrocities, ferment and fury than in any single generational rebellion in history. In this unique period

Luther and Melancthon, Zwingli and Farel, Charles V and Henry VIII, Francis I and several Popes had contended for the heart, soul and mind of Europe."[5]

The Spaniard emperor of the Holy Roman Empire, an ardent Roman Catholic, had sent over 30,000 Protestants to terrible deaths. Tens of thousands of French Huguenots were being slaughtered by the Roman Catholic monarchy of France for their Reformed Faith. Civil war was waging in the Netherlands, which were under the dominance of Philip II of Spain, husband of Bloody Mary. The Northern provinces had turned to the Reformed Faith, despite savage penalties, and Philip was determined to bring them back in line in a bloody war. The Muslim Turks had invaded Eastern Europe and extended their reign from Hungary and the Ukraine to Egypt and Persia, and from close to Gibraltar to the Caspian Sea. These Turks clawed at the coasts of Italy and Spain until the important sea battle in the Bay of Lepanto on October 7, 1571, when they were pushed back.

During the last decade of Elizabeth I's reign, the printed page—filled with the English language instead of Latin—swept away the medieval age and culture. As historian Otto Scott has observed:

> *Extraordinary energies were released, most strikingly in the theater, but in every branch of literature and knowledge. Discoveries in navigation were printed in English, (such as Sir Walter Raleigh's*

monumental History of the World*). These changes ushered in instrument-makers and special craftsmen who laid the basis for the industrial revolution. These were all changes attendant upon the Reformation of religion… But England, safe from invasion, was the more concentrated arena. Its changes were relatively free from interruptions. The religious fervor of the Reformation lifted the faith and the people from the decadence of the Renaissance into levels higher than mankind had every known.[6]*

THE REIGNS OF JAMES I AND CHARLES I

When Queen Elizabeth died, King James VI of Scotland was made King James I of England (1603-1625). He was the first of four Stuart kings. Although given the best Reformed education available as a child, his tutor being the great George Buchanan, James proved to be an arrogant homosexual and tyrant in both church and state as he sought to impose his will upon both. Believing in the divine right of kings—that the king's will is not only above the law, but that the king's will is the law—he endeavored to bring the English, and especially the Scottish Church which was Presbyterian and Reformed, under his domination.

James died a miserable death, and his son Charles I took the throne (1625-1649). Charles had a more noble character than James, but he inherited from his father an "aggravated form of his despotic principles, favoritism, duplicity and fondness for kingcraft."[7] As William Maxwell Hetherington has described, Charles was:

> Narrow-minded and obstinate, impatient of advice except when it coincided with his own notions, bigoted in religious matters, entertaining the most despotic ideas of his royal prerogative, and so full of dissimulation [deceit], that neither his word nor the most solemn treaties could bind him… and his most trusted counselors were his father's recent courtiers of sycophants and oppressors. His marriage to Henrietta, daughter of the French king, and a zealous Papist, caused an additional ground of jealousy, lest persons of that religious persuasion should obtain undue and pernicious influence… Instead of relaxing the severe and persecuting measures under which the Puritans had so long groaned, Charles, instigated by Laud, Bishop of London, afterwards Archbishop of Canterbury, continued to oppress that body of excellent men with increasing severity.[8]

The Nature of English Puritanism

Cromwell himself cannot be rightly understood without a concise explanation of English Puritanism.

Puritanism was that movement in the sixteenth and seventeenth centuries in England that strove for a more complete reformation and renewal of the church in England than the Tudor and Stuart monarchies allowed. The word "Puritan" was originally a contemptuous word of abuse which applied to at least five overlapping groups of people in England between 1564 and the end of the 1600s: (1) Those ministers who had serious problems with some of the ceremonies and phraseology of the *Book of Common Prayer* as smacking of Roman Catholicism; (2) those advocates for the complete reform of the Church of England along Presbyterian lines, led by Thomas Cartwright in the Sixteenth Century; (3) the faithful ministers and members of the Church of England who were "Nonconformists" because they would not conform to the king's required oaths and liturgical forms, and who practiced a serious and consistent Calvinistic piety; (4) the strict and thorough-going Calvinists who applauded the Synod of Dort and its strong doctrinal confession of the Reformed Faith in the refutation of Arminianism; (5) and those Members of Parliament and other gentry who showed deep and public respect for the things of God revealed in the Bible, the laws of England, and the liberties of the English people.

When the Protestant Reformation hit England, it created Puritanism, the goal of which was "to finish reshaping Anglican worship, to introduce effective church discipline into Anglican parishes, to establish righteousness in the political, domestic and socioeconomic fields, to convert all Englishmen to a vigorous evangelical faith. Through the preaching and teaching of the gospel and the sanctifying of all arts, sciences and skills, England was to become a land of saints, a model and paragon of corporate godliness, and as such a means of blessing to the world."[9]

J.I. Packer explains its core drive as follows:

> Puritanism was at heart a spiritual movement passionately concerned with God and godliness.... [It] was essentially a movement for church reform, pastoral renewal and evangelism, and spiritual revival; and in addition—indeed, as a direct expression of its zeal for God's honor—it was a worldview, a total Christian philosophy.[10]

Gary North has made this important observation about Puritanism's aims:

> The heart of the Puritan movement was a concept of a "clean sweep". They were not perfectionists. They rejected the idea that sinful men could, in fact, ever expect to accomplish a perfectly clean sweep of Satan's kingdom, any more than a sane woman ever expects to get her home completely free of dust and dirt, especially where there is a family growing up. But at the same time, they knew that God's ideal is an ethical clean sweep, and that it is the task of Christians to keep at those brooms (or vacuum

cleaners) daily, doing all they can to get the society swept. The ideal of the clean sweep is a perpetual one, the Puritans declared, which is why they were called Puritans. They wanted purity, not just in the church, but in the kingdom—a kingdom that encompassed far more than the heart, the family and the institutional church."[11]

THE CHARACTER OF OLIVER CROMWELL

Oliver Cromwell(1599-1658), the Lord Protector of England, Scotland, and Ireland, was born into a moderately wealthy and influential family that was thoroughly Puritan in its faith, worldview, and life. He married Elizabeth Bourchier on August 22, 1620, and for the next ten years lived in relative obscurity, busying himself "in farming, and in industrial and social duties, living as his father before him had lived.... At the time when popery was thus reappearing at the court of England, the Gospel was flourishing in the house of Oliver, who was occupied with his flocks and fields, his children, the interests of his neighbors, and above all in putting into practice the commandments of God."[12]

Being a genuine Puritan, Cromwell was not only Calvinistic in his faith and worldview, he was godly in his life. D'Aubigne observes:

> *All who were about him bore testimony to his piety.... Every day of his life he retired to read the*

Scriptures and to pray. Those who watched him
[closely] relate that after having perused a chapter in
the Bible, he was wont to prostrate himself with his
face on the ground, and with tears pour out his soul
before God.[13]

Cromwell's letters to his children are moving evidences
of his true godliness. On October 25, 1646, he wrote this
letter to his daughter:

Dear Heart, press on; let not thy husband, let not
anything cool thy affections after Christ. I hope he
[thy husband] will be an occasion to inflame them.
That which is best worthy of love in thy Husband is
that of the image of Christ he bears. Look on that,
and love it best, and all the rest for that. I pray for
thee and him; do so for me.[14]

THE INTRODUCTION OF CROMWELL INTO PUBLIC POLITICS

Cromwell was elected to Parliament in 1628. The first
time he spoke before this body was on February 11, 1629.
He was thirty years old. An eyewitness wrote of this
occasion:

All eyes were turned upon him, and the House
listened to him with attention. He wore a plain
cloth suit, which seemed to have been made by a
bad country tailor; his linen was not of the purest

white; his ruffles were old-fashioned; his hat was without a band; his sword stuck close to his side; his countenance was swollen and reddish; his voice was sharp and untunable; but his delivery was warm and animated; his frame, although exceeding the average height, strong and well-proportioned; he had a manly air, a bright and sparkling eye, and a stern look.[15]

Cromwell's first speech was against the re-establishment of Roman Catholicism in England which was a continual and real threat to the Protestant church and society of England. From the beginning of his public life to its end, Cromwell was consistent and was faithful to the one idea which he proclaimed from the housetops: Christ is the King of England, not man. Only with that confession put into practice will she by free and blessed of God.

King Charles I dissolved this Parliament immediately after the passage of a resolution by Sir John Eliot which called for these bold measures: (1) The outlawing of Arminian innovations to the doctrine of the church; (2) The outlawing of Roman Catholic rituals and submission to the pope; (3) The outlawing of the king's levying of certain taxes, with the declaration that all who levied or paid such taxes were guilty of high treason.

After Charles dissolved this Parliament, he did not call another one for eleven years, a period known as the "eleven years of tyranny." Oliver went back to his home during this time, not knowing that he was destined to lead England's resistance against Charles and to overthrow tyranny in his nation.

THE TYRANNY OF CHARLES I AND CROMWELL'S RESPONSE

The tyranny of Charles I in church and state, the oppression of English Puritanism and Scottish Presbyterianism by Archbishop Laud, the conspiracies of Charles I and Thomas Wentworth (the Earl of Strafford), regarding the use of an Irish Catholic and pagan army against Englishmen, and the other bloody plots and dishonesties of Charles were more than Cromwell and the Puritan Parliament could stand. But it was the mutilation, imprisonment, and martyrdom of godly men ordered by Laud under Charles I who dared to speak out against the restoration of the practices and ceremonies of popery that filled Cromwell's soul with particular horror and anguish.

Charles I always needed money for something, especially to finance his Irish army led by Wentworth. Therefore, in 1640 he was driven to recall Parliament so he could convince them to finance his wars. But the Puritans of Parliament were in no mood to be deceived and to place themselves, along with Protestantism and the freedom of the English people, in jeopardy. Once convened, they began to prosecute the traitorous persecutors of the

English people—Wentworth was arrested and executed as a public enemy, as was Archbishop Laud. The engines of tyranny were being dismantled. And to protect itself against the king, his conspiracies, and his army, Parliament called for the organization of a parliamentary army for the preservation of liberty and Protestantism in England. The English nobles rallied to the king, and it was at this time that the names "Cavaliers" and "Roundheads" first began to distinguish the two armies, the latter deriving their title from the shortness of their hair which was cut close about their ears.

Charles began his attack on January 3, 1642, by charging five of the most influential leaders of the House of Commons with treason. The next day, four hundred of the king's armed soldiers marched upon Parliament to arrest these men, but they received word and escaped. The civil war had begun.

Cromwell was now forty-two years old and the father of six children: Oliver, Richard, Henry, Bridget, Elizabeth, and Mary. He was living quietly at home on his lands, not thinking of raising arms against the king, like most godly landowners of his day. But he was soon forced to realize that new times called for new measures, especially when these men heard reports of the massacre of 50,000 to 200,000 Protestants in Ireland with the King's involvement; of the king's insincerity, deceitfulness and conspiracies against the English people; of the popery of the Queen and the semi-Romanism of the king; of the persecutions in Scotland; of the daily banishment of the best Christians in England; and, finally, of the threatening position that an Irish, Catholic, and pagan army posed as it positioned itself to invade England in order to advance the tyranny of the king. D'Aubigne explains:

> When everything seemed to announce that the Protestants of England would ere long be either trampled down by Popery or massacred by the sword, these serious men arose, and called upon the king, through the Commons, not to deceive the expectations of his subjects. But when they found that prince, deaf to their prayers, raising troops to overawe the Parliament, and already victorious in several encounters, they resolved in a spirit of devotedness, to save with God's assistance their country and their faith, by withdrawing from their families and exposing their lives in arms.
>
> Oliver now exchanged his parliamentary career for another that had become more necessary. The Huntingdonshire yeoman, who had given the Commons some proofs of his eloquence, was about to astonish the army still more by his courage and genius. The fervent orator was not to show himself a great general, and to become the greatest statesman of modern times.... Ere long, in his military and political career, he was to make himself known to the

world as the greatest man of his age, but at the same time a godly Christian.[16]

In order to protect the Reformation, the Puritan and Presbyterian Parliament and the English people from the treasonous tyranny of the king, Cromwell gathered thousands of godly men and created the New Model Army. He made officers out of men "not such as were... men of estate, but such as were common men, poor and of mean parentage, only he would give them the title of Godly, precious men. That was revolutionary, and it was to change the world. It was not introduced by French Jacobins or Russian Marxists, but by an English Calvinist. It was Cromwell who saw value in tradesmen, artisans, farmers and even laborers..."[17]

Richard Baxter, one of the greatest Presbyterian ministers of the century, and a royalist, but whom Cromwell made a chaplain, said that from the start Cromwell "had a special care to get religious men into his troops" because these were the sort of men he esteemed and loved; and from this happy choice flowed "the avoidings of those disorders, mutinies, plunderings and grievances of the country which debased men in armies are commonly guilty of."[18]

Cromwell said of his army: "I will raise men who will have the fear of God before their eyes, and who will bring some conscience to what they do; and I promise you they shall not be beaten."[19]

And they were not! D'Aubigne writes:

> *Cromwell's moral and religious character manifested itself in the army, and so soon as he was surrounded with persons animated by the same faith…. he passed his leisure hours in singing psalms with the officers and soldiers who participated in his religious convictions, and in attending with them on the preaching of the Word.*[20]

THE ISSUES AND CHALLENGES CROMWELL FACED

A. *The English Sects*

The two great problems that plagued Cromwell, which, after his death opened the door for the return of the Stuart kings and the renewed oppression of Protestantism, were: First, the Levelers and the other sects, such as the Fifth Monarchy men and the Diggers, called such because they set about digging in the earth of common land, calling for an end to private property and to all social distinctions. The Levelers, led by John Lilburne and John Wildman, believed that every man in England had the right to elect his representative in Parliament, but what Cromwell wanted was "rule by virtuous, selected men of standing." Although Cromwell and the Army, being Independents, not Presbyterians, had sympathy with some of these sects, the Levelers agenda went too far:

> *Cromwell was repelled by the sweeping nature of Leveler proposals. It would overturn, he observed, virtually the entire matter of government.... He believed and others believed that a man without any more than fixed property than what "he may carry about with him," a man who is "here today and gone tomorrow," would be enabled, by numbers, to enact confiscatory laws.... This debate carried matters almost to the brink; it is remarkable that Cromwell was able to moderate the debate.... Cromwell... agreed that men who had fought should have the vote.... To expand the vote to all... might be to lose all; the people might vote the king back in power.*[21]

Cromwell wanted a republic, and like America's Virginian Founding Fathers, an aristocratic one—never a democracy.

B. *The English and Scottish Royalists*

The second problem that plagued Cromwell was that the Presbyterians and Anglicans in England and Scotland were by and large monarchists who longed for the return of a legal king in England. The nationalism of many of the Scots overcame their Calvinistic theology which lead to an attempt to put Charles Stuart II on the throne. Otto Scott explains this tension:

> *Royalist insurrections blazed on every side... London rioted. A cry of "God save the king," arose,*

and the long affinity between the Stuarts and the theater, the poets and the ballad-singers began to make itself felt.... Meanwhile the Presbyterians made common cause with Arminians against the Independents and the New Model Army.[22]

With this in view, it becomes apparent why Cromwell had to oppose their efforts and deal harshly with them. His reasoning was clear: The return of the Stuart monarchy would lead to the renewed and bloody persecution of Presbyterianism in Scotland and Puritanism in England. If the gains of the Reformation were to be secured and advanced, the Protectorate, with its republicanism, must be kept in place and defended against all who would oppose it.

This being said, it must also be noted that not all Scottish Presbyterians sided with the Stuarts. After Cromwell defeated the royalist army and invaded Scotland, making the Scottish royalist army surrender, he was joined by many Scottish Presbyterians, "who gave him a magnificent reception in Edinburgh."[23]

C.   The Trial and Execution of King Charles I

On November 7, 1648, the New Model Army declared that Charles had betrayed his trust, calling for his trial. Later, Cromwell agreed.

These godly men who loved England, freedom and Christ, and the Reformed Faith saw no other choice. The Scots, because of their nationalism and monarchialism, could not be trusted, and the king and his supporters could not be trusted. And Parliament, with its Presbyterian majority, was largely unreliable. D'aubigne writes:

> Thy saw that, unless they interfered, Charles, popery and tyranny would resume the superiority; that good men would be oppressed, they themselves beheaded, their brethren compelled to flee by the thousands, if they could, into the wilds of America, and the would-be Protestant church crushed. One alternative offered itself to them. Must they abandon what they have done and let things take their course? Or must they interfere irregularly in those irregular times, and once more rescue England and the Church?... The liberties and Protestantism of England were on the verge of shipwreck, when Cromwell intervened; and all his life he upheld in Great Britain religious liberty and national prosperity.[24]

This decision to try the king was preceded by three days of prayer by the leaders of the army, including Cromwell. The trial began on Monday, January 8, 1648, in the ancient Westminster palace. The actual proceedings began the afternoon of January 20, 1648.

The king appeared dressed in black. He kept on his tall black hat, a mark of disrespect. The indictment was read. Its essence was that Charles "had been trusted with a limited power to govern by, and according to the laws of the land, and not otherwise." He had, however, conceived "a wicked design to erect and uphold in himself an unlimited and tyrannical power to rule according to his will and to overthrow the Rights and Liberties of the People." In the pursuit of this aim he had "traitorously and maliciously levied war against the present parliament and the people therein represented." "He was therefore responsible for all the evils of those wars. Finally, it concluded that "the said Charles Stuart [be impeached] as a Tyrant, Traitor and Murderer, and a public and implacable enemy to the Commonwealth of England. [Charles] laughed when the words, tyrant, traitor and murderer were read."[25]

Finally, on January 27, 1648 at 10am, the king was brought in to hear his sentence. The moderator made this summation to the king in answer to charges that the trial was unprecedented, calling on the oldest traditions in Christendom:

> *There is a contract and bargain made between the king and his people, and your oath is taken; and certainly, Sir, the bond is reciprocal, for as you are the lord, they are your liege subjects... the Bond or Protection... is due from the sovereign; the other is the Bond of Subjection that is due from the subject. Sir, if this bond is ever broken farewell sovereignty.*[26]

Instead of protecting his own subjects, Charles I had made war on them; and he thus deserved to die as tyrant, traitor, and murderer.

On the morning of Tuesday, January 30, 1648, Charles Stuart, king of England, put on two shirts so he would not shiver from the cold and give the impression of fear on the way to his execution. He did not arrive at the appointed place, outside the Banqueting Hall of Whitehall, until 2pm. All was prepared.

> The watchers held their breaths, the king stretched out his hands, the executioner swung his ax, the head fell off. A 17 year old boy among the spectators later said, the people let out "such a groan as I never heard before, and desire I may never hear again."[27]

The world has never been the same since.

D. The War with Ireland

Merle D'Aubigne puts Cromwell's war with Ireland in helpful perspective:

> The Irish Roman Catholics had broken out into rebellion, and massacred an incredible number of Protestants, estimates varying, according to different accounts, from 50,000 to 200,000. It was the Irish St. Bartholomew...[28]
>
> "On all sides," writes a great historian [Guizot], "the Protestants of Ireland were attacked unawares,

ejected from their houses, hunted down, slaughter,
exposed to all perils, all the tortures that religious
and patriotic hatred could invent ... A half-savage
people, passionately attached to its barbarism, ...
eager to avenge in a day ages of outrage and misery,
with a proud joy committed excesses which struck
their ancient masters with horror and dismay."

In fact, the Catholics burnt the houses of the
Protestants, turned them out naked in the midst of
winter, and drove them, like herds of swine, before
them. If ashamed of their nudity, and desirous of
seeking shelter from the rigor of a remarkably severe
season, these unhappy wretches took refuge in a
barn, and concealed themselves under the straw;
the rebels instantly set fire to it and burned alive.
At other times they were led without clothing to be
drowned in rivers; and if, on the road, they did not
move quick enough, they were urged forward at the
point of the pike. When they reached the river, or the
sea, they were precipitated into it in bands of several
hundreds, which is doubtless an exaggeration. If
these poor wretches rose to the surface of the water,
men were stationed along the brink to plunge them in
again with the butts of their muskets, or to fire at and
kill them. Husbands were cut to pieces in presence
of their wives; wives and virgins were abused in the
sight of their nearest relations; and infants of seven
or eight years were hung before the eyes of their

parents. Nay, the Irish even went so far as to teach their own children to strip and kill the children of the English and dash out their brains against the stones. Numbers of Protestants were buried alive, as many as seventy in one trench....

Cruel fighting, desperate violence, and frightful misery, afflicted the unhappy land [of Ireland] during eight years. Armies, or savage hordes, rather, full of hatred, disobedience, and cruelty, met and fought. Murder, pillage, conflagration wasted the most fertile parts of Ireland. Cromwell was destined to restore order and peace, and give to that country a prosperity which it had not known for many a year.[29]

Cromwell knew that if he "took prompt and formidable measures, such as were calculated to spread terror on every side, he would check the disease. If, on the other hand, he proceeded with a light and hesitating hand, he would prolong it indefinitely. To Cromwell the most energetic way appeared the most humane.... On the approach of the general of the English republic, all the parties that ravaged Ireland had united. Catholics of different shades, Episcopalian and Presbyterian Royalists, [along with many outright pagans] had rallied around [the Marquis] Ormond's standard."[30]

Only two towns, Dublin and Londonderry held for the Commonwealth of Cromwell, and they were besieged by the enemy. D'Aubigne notes:

> The success of the republican army was [colossal and monumental]. "Oliver descended on Ireland," says Carlyle, "like the hammer of Thor; smote it, as at one fell stroke, into dust and ruin, never to reunite against him more."[31]

D'Aubigne later observes:

> Historians, even those most opposed to Cromwell, acknowledge that no statesman ever did so much as he for the good of that poor country [Ireland]. Public order and security, such as had not been known for many years, revived. The province of Connaught, then a vast desert district, was soon changed into a fruitful country, and the rest of Ireland was everywhere cultivated with activity and confidence. In the space of little more than two years, the whole kingdom was covered with elegant and useful buildings, fine plantations and new enclosures. Peace, ease, and industry had returned to that unhappy land.[32]

Tom Reilly, in his book, *Cromwell: An Honorable Enemy*, defends Oliver Cromwell for his war in Ireland:

> Many of the defending forces that were killed were civilian volunteers in military posture. Cromwell's entire Irish mission was fought on a

*purely military basis, and it is to his enormous credit
that he never once departed from those parameters.
These facts have been in the public domain for some
years. Yet, as unpalatable revisionism, they appear
to be condemned to the dusty shelves of academic
obscurity.*[33]

Cromwell was not content to use the sword against
Ireland; he also sought to instruct them and convert them
with the pen. In answer to the popish manifesto from
Ireland in 1649, he wrote his *Declaration*, which is one
of the most remarkable documents ever composed by a
soldier. His was such a powerful Protestant voice, "the
likes of which, perhaps, was not heard in the seventeenth
century."[34] Because he understood that Roman priests
and their theology made Ireland the superstitious
and violent nation it was, he longed for it to be free of
Romanism and converted to Christ and His Reformed
religion.

E. *The War with Scotland*

Although Scottish Presbyterians had resisted the
tyranny of Charles I and the tyranny of Rome, after the
execution of their Scottish son, King Charles I, the Scots
"retarded their steps and put themselves in opposition
to the Commonwealth of England."[35] Cromwell and the
English Parliament had executed their Stuart because
of what the Scots saw as the usurpation of power. This

left the Scottish throne also vacant. Therefore, after they forced Charles II to sign the Solemn League and Covenant, they recognized him as the lawful heir to the throne and sought to make him king instead of Cromwell. (Charles II was, like his mother, Roman Catholic in his sentiments.) In response, Cromwell was compelled to take his New Model Army into Scotland to put down the royalist rebellion against the republic. D'Aubigne explains:

> Cromwell's feelings, as he marched against Scotland, were different from those which had led him to Ireland. To him the people were brethren— brethren who had gone astray when they invited over the licentious Charles II. That country was afterwards to feel, by 28 years of horrible persecution from 1660-1688, that the Protector was not deceived. Oliver determined to do all in his power to restore Scotland to herself…. Cromwell made a distinction between two factions he found in Scotland—the Malignants, who supported Charles Stuart, and who were as dissolute and as popishly inclined as himself; and the godly people of the nation, the true Presbyterians….Perhaps there never was a general at the head of an army, who entertained a more cordial affection towards his enemies. He had shown this at his very entrance into Scotland. The inhabitants of Dunbar being in great distress for

lack of provisions, he distributed among them peas and wheat to the value of 240 pounds. [36]

During his stay in Glasgow, Cromwell attended worship services in the Presbyterian Churches. When he attended the various churches the Scottish, ministers did not hesitate to pray for the king and call Oliver a usurper. He did not punish them in any way; on the contrary, he sought earnestly to be reconciled with them.

Cromwell commissioned several of the most godly men in Scotland to arrange the affairs of the church in Scotland. It was his desire that in the election of ministers and elders—the godliest men in the church—be chosen.

William Maxwell Hetherington remarks: "Throughout the whole of Scotland, during the period of Cromwell's domination, there prevailed a degree of civil peace beyond what had almost ever before been experienced."[37] Kirkton writes: "There were more souls converted to Christ in that short period of time, than in any season since the Reformation..."[38]

D'Aubigne summarizes:

Thus the result of Cromwell's campaign, both in Ireland and in Scotland was the peace and prosperity of those two countries. There were few wars recorded in history which have produced such beneficial consequences.[39]

THE CONTRIBUTION OF OLIVER CROMWELL: THE VISION OF A CHRISTIAN REPUBLIC

Cromwell's life was dedicated to the realization of his vision of a Christian constitutional republic in England in the place of the tyranny of the Stuart monarchs. One of the most important reforms Cromwell made was the production of England's first and last written constitution, "The Instrument of Government."

First, under Cromwell's constitution, the executive office was elective and its powers limited by a Council and by Parliament. Cromwell saw himself as a constitutional ruler. Here we see the limitation and separation of powers of civil government later so essential to the U.S. Constitution.

Second, voting privileges were restricted to owners of property, real and personal, to the value of two hundred pounds. The county representation in Parliament quadrupled, and the borough representation was halved.

Third, the "Instrument of Government" "was meant to establish a system of constitutional checks and balances which would prevent either the executive, or the Parliament, or the Council of State from becoming omnipotent."[40]

Similar to the original intent of the First Amendment to the United States Constitution:

> ... *liberty of conscience was guaranteed in the Instrument, for while "the Christian religion, as contained in the Scriptures," was to "be held forth and recommended as the public profession of these nations... none were to be compelled by penalties or otherwise." Every person might practice his own brand of Christianity "provided this liberty" were "not extended to Popery and Prelacy nor to such as, under the profession of Christ, hold forth and practice licentiousness."*[41]

The Defender of the Reformed Faith

Cromwell and the New Model Army not only swept away the tyranny of the Stuart monarchy for a time, it obtained such a reputation that the very threat of the army would end the persecution of Protestants throughout Europe. D'Aubigne explains:

> *Cromwell was not satisfied with merely frightening the pope in his own Babylon, and with directing his efforts in every quarter against the Roman power; he at the same time zealously pursued the great cause of the Reformation in Europe and in the world, and thus assigned to England that station as Queen of the Protestant world.*[42]

Cromwell had the same love for Reformed Churches all over the world as he did for those in Great Britain.

A. *The Waldensians*

On June 3, 1655, the sad news reached Cromwell from the Piedmont that filled all Protestant hearts with grief. The descendants of the Waldensians, those great Presbyterian and Reformed evangelists of the Middle Ages, were living in the valleys of Lucerne, Peroza, and St. Martin, between Piedmont and Savoy. This very year a brutal persecution of inconceivable violence broke out against them. The pope precipitated this terrible event when he announced that the country of the Waldensians would be given to the Irish who were banished for their role in the earlier massacre of the Protestants in Ireland.

Waldensian families were ordered off their family lands. They were given twenty days to prove that they either had become Roman Catholic or had sold their property to Catholics.

Many hundreds of families were compelled to flee in the midst of the rigors of winter. In the spring an army of 15,000 men entered their valleys. Twenty-two villages were reduced to ashes; aged people of both sexes were burnt in their houses; the men were hewn in pieces; the women were impaled naked; children were torn from their mothers' arms, and their brains dashed out against the rocks. One hundred and fifty females were beheaded, and there heads were used in a game of bowls....In this terrible desolation the poor inhabitants of the valleys first looked to God, and then to England. Their eyes were turned towards the Protector... [43]

When Cromwell received this sad news, he burst into tears. The historian Vaughan elaborates:

That very day he was to sign a treaty with France; but he refused to do so until the king and Mazarin had bound themselves to assist him in seeing justice done to these unfortunate inhabitants of the valleys. He sent them two thousand pounds from his own purse, and John Milton was employed to address letters to all the Protestant states of Europe.... Finally he appointed a day of fasting and humiliation, and a general collection all over England. The contribution amounted to over 37,000 pounds, a very large sum for that period.[44]

D'Aubigne notes:

As soon as it was known on the continent that Cromwell took the interests of the Waldensians so much to heart, the persecutors began to feel the greatest alarm. The Piedmontese, and their allies, already fancied they saw an English army landing from their ships and overrunning their country [in rescue of the Waldensians] ... This was Cromwell's intention..."[45]

Cromwell sought to enlist all the heads of state of Europe and their armies, if necessary, against the persecutors, if they did not cease and desist. "The zeal of the English chief was crowned with success."[46] Even the French wrote the Piedmontese, urging them to restore religious liberty to the Waldensians. D'Aubigne explains:

> There was not a potentate in Europe so bold as to dare expose himself to Cromwell's displeasure by refusing his request.
>
> At the same time this Defender of the Protestant faith, wishing to give the pope and the petty princes of Italy a lesson calculated to strike them with terror, gave out, that as he was satisfied they had been the promoters of this persecution, he would keep it in mind, and lay hold of the first opportunity to send his fleet into the Mediterranean to visit... parts of the ecclesiastical territories, and that the sound of his canon should be heard in Rome itself. He further declared publicly that he would not allow the true faith to be insulted in any part of the world.
>
> In his eyes (and he was one of the most clear-sighted of statesmen), this was not merely an isolated attack against Protestantism, but the first step of a general conspiracy which had for its object the annihilation of the reformed faith... [47]

B. The French Huguenots

Cromwell showed the same zeal for the Huguenots as he had shown for the Waldensians. From the beginning of the English Revolution led by Cromwell, the oppressed and long persecuted Huguenots had looked to their British brethren with hope for defense.

Cromwell sent his agents into France and urged the government to come out in favor of the oppressed Huguenots. The French pastors on public days of prayer prayed openly for the preservation of the Protector, calling him plainly, "their only hope, next to God." His wise diplomacy prevailed. "Marazin, influenced by his awe of Cromwell, took care that the edicts in favor of the Protestants should be observed with exactitude till then unknown."[48] It was said that this cardinal Marazin was more afraid of Cromwell than of the devil.

C. The Rest of Europe

D'Aubigne summarizes Cromwell's defense of Protestantism across Europe:

> His attachment to the great cause of Evangelical Protestantism extended all over Europe. In Switzerland, for instance, he endeavored to arouse and reanimate the interests of the Reformation.... He interposed in Germany in defense of the religious liberty of the Reformed states.... Collections

were made by his order in behalf of the persecuted Protestants of Bohemia and again in 1657 when delegates from the Polish and Silesian Protestants arrived in England complaining of the persecutions directed against them, public subscriptions were immediately opened in their favor throughout the whole country.

Cromwell conceived the idea of a great institution in favor of the evangelical faith. He proposed to unite all the various members of the Protestant body, and by this means place them in a condition to resist Rome, which was at that time preparing for conquest. To this end he resolved to found a council for the General Interests of Protestantism.... He divided the Protestant world out of England into four provinces.... The council was to consist of seven members and four secretaries, who were to keep up a correspondence with all the world, and inquire into the state of religion everywhere, to the intent that England might suitably direct her encouragement, her protection, and her support. The yearly sum of 10,000 pounds ... was to be placed at the disposal of the council.

Such was the Protector's activity. In every place he showed himself the true Samaritan, binding up the wounds of those who had fallen into the hands of the wicked, and pouring in oil and wine. He was the greatest Protestant that has lived since the days of

Calvin and Luther. More than any other sovereign of England, he deserved the glorious title of Defender of the Faith…. Rarely has there appeared in the world a heart that beat so strongly for everlasting truth.[49]

D. The Death of Oliver Cromwell

What became of England after Cromwell's death? His son succeeded him but was incapable of holding the Commonwealth together, and so, under the pressure of the royalists and traitors to the Commonwealth, the Stuart dynasty was restored to the throne of England, Scotland, and Ireland in the person of Charles II.

> *The Stuarts returned; and "when the rejoicings were over…then…the punishments followed," [as Cromwell had warned]. One hundred corpses were exhumed, among which were the great Oliver, his old and venerable mother, his dearly beloved daughter, Bridget Pym, and the famous Admiral Blake. Their mouldering bodies were hung on the three corners of the gallows at Tyburn, and the cavaliers found a subject of merriment and pleasantry in this revolting exhibition. Ears were cut off, noses were slit, and numbers lost their heads on the scaffold. The sentence pronounced against them all was conceived in the following terms: "You shall be drawn on a hurdle to the place of execution, and there you shall be hanged by the neck; and being alive, you shall be cut down and mutilated; your entrails shall be taken*

out of your body, and the same to be burnt before your eyes; and your head to be cut off, and your body to be divided into four quarters." The Stuarts, as if this were not enough, filled the country with immorality ... Two thousand ministers were driven from their benefices; the churches were oppressed; the noblest hearts of the country were forced to seek a refuge in distant lands; vast colonies in America were peopled by them; and England would have become like Spain, and worse than Spain, had not William III resumed the task so energetically begun by Cromwell.[50]

On September 3, 1658, Oliver Cromwell died. The sorrow and grief of the Protector's family, friends, and the majority of the nation cannot adequately be described. Most of the monarchs of Europe went into mourning.

It is seldom that a great man is a Christian; but Cromwell was both. The result has been that men of the world have scouted him as a hypocrite. —What most distinguishes Cromwell above all great men, and especially above all statesmen, is the predominance in him—not only in his person, but also in his government—a solidly Reformed and Biblical theology, worldview and way of life. He thought that the political and national greatness of Great Britain could not be established in a firm and lasting manner, unless the pure and unmixed Gospel of Jesus Christ was preached to the people and unless a truly Christian life flowed through the veins of the whole nation.[51]

I conclude this sketch of Oliver Cromwell with this prayer that those gathered in his bedroom heard him pray shortly before his death:

Lord, though I am a miserable and wretched creature, I am in covenant with Thee through grace. And I may, I will come to Thee for Thy people. Thou hast made me, though very unworthy, a mean instrument to do them some good, and Thee service; and many of them have set too high a value upon me, though others wish and would be glad of my death; Lord, however Thou dispose of me, continue and go on to do good for them. Pardon Thy foolish people! Forgive their sins and do not forsake them, but love and bless them. Give them consistency of judgment, one heart, and mutual love; and go on to deliver them, and with the work of reformation; and make the name of Christ glorious in the world. Teach those who look too much on Thy instruments, to depend more upon Thyself. Pardon such as desire to trample upon the dust of a poor worm; for they are Thy people too. And pardon the folly of this short prayer. And give me rest for Jesus Christ's sake, to whom, with Thee and Thy Holy Spirit, be all honor and glory, now and forever! Amen.[52]

APPENDIX B

The HISTORY and IMPACT of the GENEVA BIBLE

by Dr. Marshall Foster

T he Geneva Bible has been the lost treasure of Christendom for almost four centuries. Nearly forgotten by the modern world, this version of the Holy Scriptures was researched, compiled, and translated into English by exiled Reformers in Geneva, Switzerland, between 1557 and 1560, and was destined to be the major component of the English-speaking people's rise from the backwaters of history to the center of civilization.

This edition of the Geneva Bible is the first completely

new publication since the time of its first issue, and timed for release on the 400th anniversary of the settlement of Jamestown in what is now Virginia. The Geneva Bible surely was carried aboard their three ships that sailed from England in December of 1606. The New England Pilgrims likewise relied on the Geneva Bible for comfort and strength on their 66-day voyage aboard the Mayflower in 1620, and were even more dependent upon it as they wrote the Mayflower Compact, a document unique in world history and the first constitutional government in the western hemisphere.

SETTING THE STAGE

England of 1557 was a society beset by contradictions, oppression, even barbarity. More than 300 men had been burned at the stake by the Catholic tyrant, "Bloody Mary" Tudor, merely for promoting the English Reformation. Many clergymen, Catholic and Protestant both, exacerbated rather than soothed the distress; semi-literate as a class, most received their parish jobs as payoffs and often were unwilling to preach, or incapable of composing sermons. The impoverished and spiritually bereft masses found solace elsewhere—sloth, dissipation, or drink—while the gentry sought after wealth, social position, and favors of royal courts.

Into this seemingly hopeless culture of corruption and error, the light of God's written Word—in the newly

translated, published, and distributed Geneva Bible—
inexorably began to liberate the English-speaking people,
penetrating hearts and transforming minds. It is no
exaggeration to say that the Geneva Bible was the most
significant catalyst of the transformation of England,
Scotland, and America from slavish feudalism to the
heights of Christian civilization.

As the first Bible to be read by the common people in
English, the Geneva Bible inspired those who championed
self-government, free enterprise, education, civic virtue,
protection of women and children, and godly culture.
John Knox preached with power from the Geneva Bible
at St. Giles Cathedral in Edinburgh, mightily influencing
Scotland's restoration from clan-dominated, semi-pagan
barbarity to Christian faith and liberty. The legendary
Soldier's Pocket Bible, famous as the spiritual companion
to Oliver Cromwell's Christian soldiers in the English civil
war, was composed of verses from the Geneva translation.
And it was the Geneva Bible that was carried and read by
the Pilgrims as they landed in the wilderness of America
and extrapolated concepts of civic morality from its pages as
they laid foundation-stones of the world's first constitutional
republic.

For more than 1500 years, an unfettered spread of
the Gospel in the world was stymied without a reliable,
written version of God's Word in the common language
of the people. Rome's missionaries and monasteries

had played their roles in civilizing the pagan tribes of Europe and establishing Christian authority. But abuse of power and perversion of truth by prelates and kings were commonplace by the Renaissance.

The providential invention of movable type, enabling not just the publication but the practical distribution of the Geneva Bible, freed God's Book from the echoes of august cathedrals and the dead Latin language into the lives and homes, hearths and hearts, of everyday people in the English-speaking world.

HISTORY OF THE GENEVA BIBLE

The Geneva translation's revolutionary impact can be better appreciated by the realization that the Bible has only been available to laymen for four hundred years. Prior to the printing of Luther's German Bible in 1534, and the Geneva Bible in English, everyday believers, regardless of nationality, never had a Bible of their own to read, study, to "hide in their hearts." The Church and kings kept all but clergy and Latin scholars from reading Scripture; in England it even became, by royal edict, a capital crime even to read the Bible in the "vulgar tongue" (the English language). In 1526, the English scholar William Tyndale attempted to translate the Bible into English and was forced to flee to Germany, where he met Martin Luther, and then to Belgium, all in an effort to translate the Bible and to fulfill the commitment made to a clergyman who attempted to dissuade him from his mission: "[God's] version was to be made for all the people, even the humblest: if God spare my life, ere many years pass I will cause the boy that driveth the plow to know more of Scripture than thou [a theologian] dost."

Fulfilling his promise, Tyndale published the first-ever mechanically printed New Testament in the English language, in 1526. Six thousand first-edition copies were smuggled to England and lit a fire that could not be extinguished.

But Tyndale was hunted, captured, and imprisoned in the Belgian town of Vilvoorde. On March 6, 1536, he was strangled and burned at the stake, his last words "Lord, open the King of England's eyes." His prayers were answered. Tyndale's monumental work made its way to some English pulpits, and one had been paid for by the same king who persecuted him, Henry VIII, who became a supporter of Protestant reformers.

These first English passages of Scripture, however, were pulpit Bibles, for use by the clergy; still the people had no Bibles they could afford... nor, for the most part, that they could read.

In 1553, upon the death of Henry VIII's sixteen-year-old Protestant son Edward, Mary Tudor ascended the throne, soon married the Catholic King of Spain, and set about, often with violent cruelty, to stamp out the Reformation. Determined to force the English people back to Roman Catholicism, she ordered the burning of all copies of the Bible in English. She caused more than four hundred reformers, pastors and Bible translators to be burned at the stake, well earning her for all of history the sobriquet Bloody Mary.

Queen Mary's vicious crusade drove approximately eight hundred English scholars to the Continent (the "Marian Exile") but God used this exodus to assemble, in Geneva, some of the finest theologians and Biblical scholars in history. Here, under the protection of John Calvin's "little republic," this special group of thinkers, led by William Whittingham (Calvin's brother-in-law) and assisted by Miles Coverdale, Christopher Goodman, Anthony Gilby, John Knox, and Thomas Sampson, produced a new English Bible not beholden to any king or prelate—The Geneva Bible,—the first English Translation from the original tongues since Tyndale's revised New Testament of 1534. The reformers sought to produce a Bible that was not based on the less-authentic Latin Vulgate promoted by Queen Mary. They researched the most recently collected Greek and Hebrew manuscripts. Whitingham's completed revision of William Tyndale's New Testament, including many annotations and commentaries, was published in 1557; and almost immediately work began on a revision of the entire Bible. Devoting more than two years of intense toil to the task, the result was the first Bible translation produced by a committee rather than by one individual. They drew upon painstaking translations from the original languages; Theodore Beza's work and other continental translations, such as Luther's; all overseen and supported by reformers like John Knox and John Calvin.

The completed Geneva Bible was published in 1560 and dedicated to Queen Elizabeth, who had succeeded her half-sister Bloody Mary to the throne and, at least for political reasons, supported a definitive break with the Church of Rome. The Geneva Bible was an instant success that captured the hearts of the people with its powerful, uncompromising prose and more than 300,000 words of annotations in the margins to aid in personal study and understanding.

This unique 2006 edition of the 1599 version of the Geneva Bible uses Tomson's revised New Testament (a later revision of Whitingham's New Testament of 1557) and Junius's annotated notes on "Revelation." The 1599 version has the most complete compilation of annotations of any of the Geneva editions. It also has a table of interpretations of proper names, which are chiefly found in the Old Testament, and a table of principle subjects contained in the Bible. The Books of Psalms were collected into English meters by Thomas Sternhold, John Hopkins, and others, to encourage their recitation in the manner of the early churches. Also included were prayers to be used by English congregations every morning and evening.

For generations after its first printing, the Geneva Bible remained the Bible of personal study in England, Scotland, and then in America. A 1579 Scottish edition of the Geneva version was the first Bible printed in Scotland; it soon became the standard of the Scottish Kirk. The Scottish Parliament required that every householder worth three hundred marks, and every yeoman or burgess worth five hundred pounds, have a Bible in the "vulgar tongue" in their homes, under penalty of ten pounds.

The Geneva Bible came to be called affectionately the "Breeches Bible." The term derives from the reference in Genesis 3:7 to Adam and Eve clothing themselves in fig-leaf "breeches," a decidedly English term.

So popular was the Geneva Bible that between 1560 and 1644 at least 144 editions were published, compared to but five editions of another, inferior, translation known as The Bishops Bible. The Geneva Bible lost its prominence only after the King James Authorized Version of 1611 was widely promoted by the King and Bishop Laud (later Archbishop of Canterbury and persecutor of Presbyterians), who outlawed the printing of the Geneva Bible in the realm. When the Geneva Bible disappeared, there were widespread complaints that people "could not see into the sense of Scripture for lack of the spectacles of those Genevan annotations."

The Uniqueness of the Geneva Bible

The Geneva Bible stands as one of the great achievements of Biblical scholarship. It is the Bible of "firsts":

- It was the first English Bible to be fully translated from the original languages. The fall of Constantinople (1453) had a providential benefit, as previously unknown Greek and Hebrew manuscripts were carried to the West by Christians fleeing the Islamic onslaught. The Renaissance Period's interest in antiquity also brought authentic documents and historical details to the attention of the Geneva scholars.

- It was the first Bible translation to be printed in easy-to-read Roman type, rather than the older "Black Face" Gothic text. The 2006 edition of the 1599 Geneva version goes a step further; while keeping the Bible text and notes accurate word-for-word with the sixteenth-century edition, spelling has been updated and the type reset in an even easier-to-read form.

- It was the first Bible to qualify as a study Bible, providing readers with copious notes, annotations, and commentary about the original manuscripts, clarification of ambiguous meanings, and cross references. It is a tribute to the intellectual integrity of the translators that they also used italics for the interpolated words that were not in the original languages—helpful for the English vernacular, and the first-ever use of this tool in historical or literary analysis.

- It was the first Bible to assign chapter demarcation, and to add verse numbers within chapters. These innovations facilitated the location of passages, memorization, and recitation… and the nurture of a nation of Bible readers.

- It was the first Bible to be printed in a small quarto edition, portable and affordable. This made it suitable for family use without expensive folios. Every Pilgrim family, for example, had a Geneva Bible as the convenient center of its daily life.

Impact of the Geneva Bible

The Geneva Bible significantly assisted the creation of the modern English language—the lingua franca of today's world. William Tyndale's linguistic genius and the poetic mastery of Miles Coverdale's earlier translation of the Poetic Books are widely credited with sparking the English literary excellence of the seventeenth and eighteenth centuries: the Geneva Bible was the Bible of William Shakespeare, John Milton, John Bunyan, the

Puritans (considered history's greatest expositors), and the Pilgrims who sailed to America. It was the Bible that John Rolfe likely would have used in the conversion of Pocahontas at Jamestown in 1611.

The impact of the annotations and commentary in the Geneva Bible cannot be underestimated. The Calvinist notes of the Geneva Bible infuriated King James I at Hampton Court in 1604, prompting him to authorize a group of Puritan scholars to produce a version of the Bible without annotation for him; ironically, the excellent Authorized Version might never have been written were it not for King James's antipathy toward the Geneva Bible.

The marginal notes of the Geneva Bible present a systematic Biblical worldview centered on the Sovereignty of God over all of His creation including churches and kings. This unique Biblical emphasis, though fraught with dangers beyond spiritual debates (i.e., political and social pressure), was one of John Calvin's great contributions to the English Reformers. For example, the marginal note in the Geneva Bible for Exodus 1:9 indicated that the Hebrew midwives were correct to disobey the Egyptian rulers. King James called such interpretations "seditious." The tyrant knew that if the people could hold him accountable to God's Word, his days as a king ruling by "Divine Right" were numbered, but Calvin and the Reformers defended the clear meaning of Scripture against whims of king or popes. Thus did the Geneva Bible begin the unstoppable march to liberty in England, Scotland, and America.

The marginal notes of the Geneva Bible also served to liberate believers from the ignorance, heresy, and tyranny of the Middle Ages. Calvin, and the Reformers who followed in his footsteps, expounded the whole counsel of God concerning doctrines of Sola Scriptura—the Word of God alone, inspired and directional for our lives and culture; Sola Fide—faith alone as the only means of justification before God; Sola Christus—Christ alone as mankind's only mediator, lord, and king; Sola Gratia—grace alone as the only hope of salvation and sanctification; and Soli Deo Gloria—God alone, not king nor pope, to receive the glory He is due in heaven and on earth.

Today, these theological "marginalia" might seem rudimentary or innocuous, but when they were systematically taught from Scripture and applied to life, as was done in the commentary in the Geneva Bible, entire nations and societies were transformed. Ultimately, the knowledge of and obedience to God's written Word led to constitutional, limited government; the end of slavery and the caste system; free enterprise and the concept of private property; the so-called Puritan work ethic that fueled the scientific and industrial revolutions; wholesome, uplifting standards in the arts;

and many other forms of progress.

The bold innovations of the Geneva Bible continue to have an impact in today's world. Because of its revolutionary format and features, the Geneva Bible became the foundation for what we call group Bible study, and was a catalyst for the acceptance of the liberating doctrine of the "priesthood of all believers." Puritan lay leaders expounded the Word and other congregants offered commentary and invited discussion—all of which, today, might be taken for granted; but such practices were previously and strictly proscribed.

THE GENEVA BIBLE'S APPLICATION FOR TODAY

The Geneva Bible providentially was unleashed upon a dark, discouraged, downtrodden English-speaking world, at a time when Christendom was in real danger of regressing to a form of Caesar-worship. A Bible appeared that created the conditions for a Christian reformation of life and culture, the likes of which the world had never seen—its hallmarks including the explosion of faith; an emphasis on integrity; a unique and vital missionary movement; creative literature, economic blessings; and political and religious freedom. By the time of the defeat of the Spanish Armada in 1588, just twenty-eight years after the first printing of the Geneva Bible, it was already being said of the English that they were becoming a "people of the Book."

Almost five hundred years later, our culture is once again desperate for the Truth. Many people have forgotten, abandoned, or rejected the great lessons of the Reformation and the Biblical theology that inspired the greatest accomplishments of Western Civilization. We fervently pray that the re-introduction of this powerful tool of Godly dominion, the Geneva Bible, will, with God's favor, light the fires for another powerful reformation. As we read this sacred volume, let us remember the sacrifice of the persecuted scholars on the shores of Lake Geneva.

John Calvin, in exile in Geneva, surrounded by pagan kings, wars, and a corrupt Roman church, said these optimistic words about the spread of God's Word:

> Whatever resistance we see today offered by almost all the world to the progress of the truth, we must not doubt that our Lord will come at last to break through all the undertakings of men and make a passage for His Word. Let us hope boldly, then, more than we can understand; He will still surpass our opinion and our hope.

May we be inspired from His Word, as our spiritual forbears were, to be fearlessly optimistic about the power of His Gospel and the furtherance of His Kingdom on earth.

For unto us a Childe is borne, and unto us a sonne is given: and the government and peace shal have none end: he shall sit upon the throne of David, and upon his kingdome, to order it, and to establish it with judgement and with justice, from hence forthe, and for ever: the zeale of the Lorde of hostes wil performe this (Isaiah 9:6-7, 1599 Geneva Bible).

APPENDIX C

The SOLEMN LEAGUE
and COVENANT

Asolemn league and covenant for Reformation and Defence of Religion, the honour and happiness of the King, and the peace and safety of the three kingdoms of England, Scotland and Ireland.

We noblemen, barons, knights, gentlemen, citizens, burgesses, ministers of the Gospel, and commons of all sorts in the kingdoms of England, Scotland and Ireland, by the providence of God living under one King, and being of one reformed religion; having before our eyes the glory of God, and the advancement of the kingdom of our Lord and Saviour Jesus Christ, the honour and happiness of the King's Majesty and his posterity, and the true public liberty, safety and peace of the kingdoms, wherein every one's private condition is included; and calling to mind the treacherous and bloody plots, conspiracies, attempts and practices of the enemies of God against the true religion and professors thereof in all places, especially in these three kingdoms, ever since the reformation of religion; and how much their rage, power and presumption are of late, and at this time increased and exercised, whereof the deplorable estate of the Church and kingdom of Ireland, the distressed estate of the Church and kingdom of England, and the dangerous estate of the Church and kingdom of Scotland, are present and public testimonies: we have (now at last) after other means of supplication, remonstrance, protestations and sufferings, for the preservation of ourselves and our religion from utter ruin and destruction, according to the commendable practice of these kingdoms in former times, and the example of God's people in other nations, after mature deliberation, resolved and determined to enter into a mutual and solemn league and covenant, wherein we all subscribe, and each one of us for himself, with our hands lifted up to the most high God, do swear,

I. That we shall sincerely, really and constantly, through the grace of God, endeavour in our several places and callings, the preservation of the reformed religion in the Church of Scotland, in doctrine, worship, discipline and government, against our common enemies; the reformation of religion in the kingdoms of England and Ireland, in doctrine, worship, discipline and government, according to the Word of God, and the example of the best reformed Churches; and we shall endeavour to bring the Churches of God in the three kingdoms to the nearest conjunction and uniformity in religion, confession of faith, form of Church government, directory for worship and catechising, that we, and our posterity after us, may, as brethren, live in faith and love, and the Lord may delight to dwell in the midst of us.

II. That we shall in like manner, without respect of persons, endeavour the extirpation of Popery, prelacy (that is, Church government by Archbishops, Bishops, their Chancellors and Commissaries, Deans, Deans and Chapters, Archdeacons, and all other ecclesiastical officers depending on that hierarchy), superstition, heresy, schism, profaneness, and whatsoever shall be found to be contrary to sound doctrine and the power of godliness, lest we partake in other men's sins, and thereby be in danger to receive of their plagues; and that the Lord may be one, and His name one in the three kingdoms.

III. We shall with the same sincerity, reality and constancy, in our several vocations, endeavour with our estates and lives mutually to preserve the rights and privileges of the Parliaments, and the liberties of the kingdoms, and to preserve and defend the King's Majesty's person and authority, in the preservation and defence of the true religion and liberties of the kingdoms, that the world may bear witness with our consciences of our loyalty, and that we have no thoughts or intentions to diminish His Majesty's just power and greatness.

IV. We shall also with all faithfulness endeavour the discovery of all such as have been or shall be incendiaries, malignants or evil instruments, by hindering the reformation of religion, dividing the King from his people, or one of the kingdoms from another, or making any faction or parties amongst the people, contrary to the league and covenant, that they may be brought to public trial and receive condign punishment, as the degree of their offences shall require or deserve, or the supreme judicatories of both kingdoms respectively, or others having power from them for that effect, shall judge convenient.

V. And whereas the happiness of a blessed peace between these kingdoms, denied in former times to our progenitors, is by the good providence of God granted to us, and hath been lately concluded and settled by both Parliaments: we shall each one of us, according to our places and interest, endeavour that they may remain conjoined in a firm peace and union to all posterity, and that justice may be done upon the wilful opposers thereof, in manner expressed in the precedent articles.

VI.   We shall also, according to our places and callings, in this common cause of religion, liberty and peace of the kingdom, assist and defend all those that enter into this league and covenant, in the maintaining and pursuing thereof; and shall not suffer ourselves, directly or indirectly, by whatsoever combination, persuasion or terror, to be divided and withdrawn from this blessed union and conjunction, whether to make defection to the contrary part, or give ourselves to a detestable indifferency or neutrality in this cause, which so much concerneth the glory of God, the good of the kingdoms, and the honour of the King; but shall all the days of our lives zealously and constantly continue therein, against all opposition, and promote the same according to our power, against all lets and impediments whatsoever; and what we are not able ourselves to suppress or overcome we shall reveal and make known, that it may be timely prevented or removed: all which we shall do as in the sight of God.

And because these kingdoms are guilty of many sins and provocations against God, and His Son Jesus Christ, as is too manifest by our present distresses and dangers, the fruits thereof: we profess and declare, before God and the world, our unfeigned desire to be humbled for our own sins, and for the sins of these kingdoms;

especially that we have not as we ought valued the inestimable benefit of the Gospel; that we have not laboured for the purity and power thereof; and that we have not endeavoured to receive Christ in our hearts, nor to walk worthy of Him in our lives, which are the causes of other sins and transgressions so much abounding amongst us; and our true and unfeigned purpose, desire and endeavour, for ourselves and all others under our power and charge, both in public and in private, in all duties we owe to God and man, to amend our lives, and each one to go before another in the example of a real reformation, that the Lord may turn away His wrath and heavy indignation, and establish these Churches and kingdoms in truth and peace. And this covenant we make in the presence of Almighty God, the Searcher of all hearts, with a true intention to perform the same, as we shall answer at that Great Day when the secrets of all hearts shall be disclosed: most humbly beseeching the Lord to strengthen us by His Holy Spirit for this end, and to bless our desires and proceedings with such success as may be a deliverance and safety to His people, and encouragement to the Christian Churches groaning under or in danger of the yoke of Anti-christian tyranny, to join in the same or like association and covenant, to the glory of God, the enlargement of the kingdom of Jesus Christ, and the peace and tranquillity of Christian kingdoms and commonwealths.

APPENDIX D

ACT *of* SUPREMACY

Albeit, the King's Majesty justly and rightfully is and oweth to be the supreme head of the Church of England, and so is recognised by the clergy of this realm in their Convocations; yet nevertheless for corroboration and confirmation thereof, and for increase of virtue in Christ's religion within this realm of England, and to repress and extirp all errors, heresies and other enormities and abuses heretofore used in the same, Be it enacted by authority of this present Parliament that the King our sovereign lord, his heirs and successors kings of this realm, shall be taken, accepted and reputed the only supreme head in earth of the Church of England called

Anglicana Ecclesia, and shall have and enjoy annexed and united to the imperial crown of this realm as well the title and style thereof, as all honours, dignities, preeminences, jurisdictions, privileges, authorities, immunities, profits and commodities, to the said dignity of supreme head of the same Church belonging and appertaining. And that our said sovereign lord, his heirs and successors kings of this realm, shall have full power and authority from time to time to visit, repress, redress, reform, order, correct, restrain and amend all such errors, heresies, abuses, offences, contempts and enormities, whatsoever they be, which by any manner spiritual authority or jurisdiction ought or may lawfully be reformed, repressed, ordered, redressed corrected, restrained or amended, most to the pleasure of Almighty God, the increase of virtue in Christ's religion, and for the conservation of the peace, unity and tranquillity of this realm: any usage, custom, foreign laws, foreign authority, prescription or any other thing or things to the contrary hereof notwithstanding.

APPENDIX E

ELIZABETH'S ACT *of* UNIFORMITY (1559)

Where at the death of our late sovereign lord King Edward VI there remained one uniform order of common service and prayer, and of the administration of sacraments, rites, and ceremonies in the Church of England, which was set forth in one book, intituled: The Book of Common Prayer, and Administration of Sacraments, and other rites and ceremonies in the Church of England; authorized by Act of Parliament holden in the fifth and sixth years of our said late sovereign lord King Edward VI, intituled: An Act for the uniformity of common prayer, and administration of the sacraments; the which was repealed and taken away by Act of Parliament in the first year of the reign of our late sovereign lady Queen Mary, to the great decay of the due honour of God, and discomfort to the professors of the truth of Christ's religion:

Be it therefore enacted by the authority of this present Parliament, that the said statute of repeal, and everything therein contained, only concerning the said book, and the service, administration of sacraments, rites, and ceremonies contained or appointed in or by the said book, shall be void and of none effect, from and after the feast of the Nativity of St. John Baptist next coming; and that the said book, with the order of service, and of the administration of sacraments, rites, and ceremonies, with the alterations and additions therein added and appointed by this statute, shall stand and be, from and after the said feast of the Nativity of St. John Baptist, in full force and effect, according to the tenor and effect of this statute; anything in the aforesaid statute of repeal to the contrary notwithstanding.

And further be it enacted by the queen's highness, with the assent of the Lords (sic) and Commons in this present Parliament assembled, and by authority of the same, that all and singular ministers in any cathedral or parish church, or other place within this realm of England, Wales, and the marches of the same, or other the queen's dominions, shall from and after the feast of the Nativity of St. John Baptist next coming be bounden to say and use the Matins, Evensong, celebration of the Lord's Supper and administration of each of the sacraments, and all their common and open prayer, in such order and form as is mentioned in the said book, so authorized by Parliament in the said fifth and sixth years of the reign of King Edward VI, with one alteration or addition of certain lessons to be used on every Sunday in the year, and the form of the Litany altered and corrected, and two sentences only added in the delivery of the sacrament to the communicants, and none other or otherwise.

And that if any manner of parson, vicar, or other whatsoever minister, that ought or should sing or say common prayer mentioned in the said book, or minister the sacraments, from and after the feast of the nativity of St. John Baptist next coming, refuse to use the said common prayers, or to minister the sacraments in such cathedral or parish church, or other places as he should use to minister the same, in such order and form as they be mentioned and set forth in the said book, or shall wilfully or obstinately standing in the same, use any other rite, ceremony, order, form, or manner of celebrating of the Lord's Supper, openly or privily, or Matins, Evensong, administration of the sacraments, or other open prayers, than is mentioned and set forth in the said book (open prayer in and throughout this Act, is meant that prayer which is for other to come unto, or hear, either in common churches or private chapels or oratories, commonly called the service of the Church), or shall preach, declare, or speak anything in the derogation or depraving of the said book, or anything therein contained, or of any part thereof, and shall be thereof lawfully convicted, according to the laws of this realm, by verdict of twelve men, or by his own confession, or by the notorious evidence of the fact, shall lose and forfeit to the queen's highness, her heirs and successors, for his first offence, the profit of all his spiritual benefices or promotions coming or arising in one whole year next after his conviction; and also that the person so convicted shall for the same offence suffer imprisonment by the space of six months, without bail or mainprize.

And if any such person once convicted of any offence concerning the premises, shall after his first conviction eftsoons offend, and be thereof, in form aforesaid, lawfully convicted, that then the same person shall for his second offence suffer imprisonment by the space of one whole year, and also shall therefore be deprived, ipso facto, of all his spiritual promotions; and that it shall be lawful to all patrons or donors of all and singular the same spiritual promotions, or of any of them, to present or collate to the same, as though the person and persons so offending were dead.

And that if any such person or persons, after he shall be twice convicted in form aforesaid, shall offend against any of the premises the third time, and shall be thereof, in form aforesaid, lawfully convicted, that then the person so offending and convicted the third time, shall be deprived, ipso facto, of all his spiritual promotions, and also shall suffer imprisonment during his life.

And if the person that shall offend, and be convicted in form aforesaid, concerning any of the premises, shall not be beneficed, nor have any spiritual promotion, that then the same person so offending and convicted shall for the first offence suffer imprisonment during one whole year next after his said conviction, without bail or mainprize. And if any such person, not having any spiritual promotion, after his first conviction shall eftsoons offend in anything concerning the premises, and shall be, in form aforesaid, thereof lawfully convicted, that then the same person shall for his second offence suffer imprisonment during his life.

And it is ordained and enacted by the authority aforesaid, that if any person or persons whatsoever, after the said feast of the Nativity of St. John Baptist next coming, shall in any interludes, plays, songs, rhymes, or by other open words, declare or speak anything in the derogation, depraving, or despising of the same book, or of anything therein contained, or any part thereof, or shall, by open fact, deed, or by open threatenings, compel or cause, or otherwise procure or maintain, any parson, vicar, or other minister in any cathedral or parish church, or in chapel, or in any other place, to sing or say any common or open prayer, or to minister any sacrament otherwise, or in any other manner and form, than is mentioned in the said book; or that by any of the said means shall unlawfully interrupt or let any parson, vicar, or other minister in any cathedral or parish church, chapel, or any other place, to sing or say common and open prayer, or to minister the sacraments or any of them, in such manner and form as is mentioned in the said book; that then every such person, being thereof lawfully convicted in form abovesaid, shall forfeit to the queen our sovereign lady, her heirs and successors, for the first offence a hundred marks.

And if any person or persons, being once convicted of any such offence, eftsoons offend against any of the last recited offences, and shall, in form aforesaid, be thereof lawfully convicted, that then the same person so offending and convicted shall, for the second offence, forfeit to the queen our sovereign lady, her heirs and successors, four hundred marks.

And if any person, after he, in form aforesaid, shall have been twice convicted of any offence concerning any of the last recited offences, shall offend the third time, and be thereof, in form abovesaid, lawfully convicted, that then every person so offending and convicted shall for his third offence forfeit to our sovereign lady the queen all his goods and chattels, and shall suffer imprisonment during his life.

And if any person or persons, that for his first offence concerning the premises shall be convicted, in form aforesaid, do not pay the sum to be paid by virtue of his conviction, in such manner and form as the same ought to be paid, within six weeks next after his conviction; that then every person so convicted, and so not paying the same, shall for the same first offence, instead of the said sum, suffer imprisonment by the space of six months, without bail or mainprize. And if any person or persons, that for his second offence concerning the premises shall be convicted in form aforesaid, do not pay the said sum to be paid by virtue of his conviction and this statute, in such manner and form as the same ought to be paid, within six weeks next after his said second conviction; that then every person so convicted, and not so paying the same, shall, for the same second offence, in the stead of the said sum, suffer imprisonment during twelve months, without bail or mainprize.

And that from and after the said feast of the Nativity of St. John Baptist next coming, all and every person and persons inhabiting within this realm, or any other the queen's majesty's dominions, shall diligently and faithfully, having no lawful or reasonable excuse to be absent, endeavour themselves to resort to their parish church or chapel accustomed, or upon reasonable let thereof, to some usual place where common prayer and such service of God shall be used in such time of let, upon every Sunday and other days ordained and used to be kept as holy days, and then and there to abide orderly and soberly during the time of the common prayer, preachings, or other service of God there to be used and ministered; upon pain of punishment by the censures of the Church, and also upon pain that every person so offending shall forfeit for every such offence twelve pence, to be levied by the churchwardens of the parish where such offence shall be done, to the use of the poor of the same parish, of the goods, lands, and tenements of such offender, by way of distress.

And for due execution hereof, the queen's most excellent majesty, the Lords temporal (sic), and all the Commons, in this present Parliament assembled, do in God's name earnestly require and charge all the archbishops, bishops, and other ordinaries, that they shall endeavour themselves to the uttermost of their knowledges, that the due and true execution hereof may be had throughout their dioceses and charges, as they will answer before God, for such evils and plagues wherewith Almighty God may justly punish His people for neglecting this good and wholesome law.

And for their authority in this behalf, be it further enacted by the authority aforesaid, that all and singular the same archbishops, bishops, and all other their officers exercising ecclesiastical jurisdiction, as well in place exempt as not exempt, within their dioceses, shall have full power and authority by this Act to reform, correct, and punish by censures of the Church, all and singular persons which shall offend within any their jurisdictions or dioceses, after the said feast of the Nativity of St. John Baptist next coming, against this Act and statute; any other law, statute, privilege, liberty, or provision heretofore made, had, or suffered to the contrary notwithstanding.

And it is ordained and enacted by the authority aforesaid, that all and every justices of oyer and terminer, or justices of assize, shall have full power and authority in every of their open and general sessions, to inquire, hear, and determine all and all manner of offences that shall be committed or done contrary to any article contained in this present Act, within the limits of the commission to them directed, and to make process for the execution of the same, as they may do against any person being indicted before them of trespass, or lawfully convicted thereof.

Provided always, and be it enacted by the authority aforesaid, that all and every archbishop and bishop shall or may, at all time and times, at his liberty and pleasure, join and associate himself, by virtue of this Act, to the said justices of oyer and terminer, or to the said justices of assize, at every of the said open and general sessions to be holden in any place within his diocese, for and to the inquiry, hearing, and determining of the offences aforesaid.

Provided also, and be it enacted by the authority aforesaid, that the books concerning the said services shall, at the cost and charges of the parishioners of every parish and cathedral church, be attained and gotten before the said feast of the Nativity of St. John Baptist next following; and that all such parishes and cathedral churches, or other places where the said books shall be attained and gotten before the said feast of the Nativity of St. John Baptist, shall, within three weeks next after the said books so attained and gotten, use the said service, and put the same in use according to this Act.

And be it further enacted by the authority aforesaid, that no person or persons shall be at any time hereafter impeached or otherwise molested of or for any the offences above mentioned, hereafter to be committed or done contrary to this Act, unless he or they so offending be thereof indicted at the next general sessions to be holden before any such justices of oyer and terminer or justices of assize, next after any offence committed or done contrary to the tenor of this Act.

Provided always, and be it ordained and enacted by the authority aforesaid, that all and singular lords of the Parliament, for the third offence above mentioned, shall be tried by their peers.

Provided also, and be it ordained and enacted by the

authority aforesaid, that the mayor of London, and all other mayors, bailiffs, and other head officers of all and singular cities, boroughs, and towns corporate within this realm, Wales, and the marches of the same, to the which justices of assize do not commonly repair, shall have full power and authority by virtue of this Act to inquire, hear, and determine the offences abovesaid, and every of them, yearly within fifteen days after the feasts of Easter and St. Michael the Archangel, in like manner and form as justices of assize and oyer and terminer may do.

Provided always, and be it ordained and enacted by the authority aforesaid, that all and singular archbishops and bishops, and every their chancellors, commissaries, archdeacons, and other ordinaries, having any peculiar ecclesiastical jurisdiction. shall have full power and authority by virtue of this Act, as well to inquire in their visitation, synods, and elsewhere within their jurisdiction at any other time and place, to take occasions (sic) and informations of all and every the things above mentioned, done, committed, or perpetrated within the limits of their jurisdictions and authority, and to punish the same by admonition, excommunication, sequestration, or deprivation, and other censures and processes, in like form as heretofore has been used in like cases by the queen's ecclesiastical laws.

Provided always, and be it enacted, that whatsoever person offending in the premises shall, for the offence, first receive punishment of the ordinary, having a testimonial thereof under the said ordinary's seal, shall not for the same offence eftsoons be convicted before the justices: and likewise receiving, for the said offence, first punishment by the justices, he shall not for the same offence eftsoons receive punishment of the ordinary; anything contained in this Act to the contrary notwithstanding.

Provided always, and be it enacted, that such ornaments of the church, and of the ministers thereof, shall be retained and be in use, as was in the Church of England, by authority of Parliament, in the second year of the reign of King Edward VI, until other order shall be therein taken by the authority of the queen's majesty, with the advice of her commissioners appointed and authorized, under the great seal of England, for causes ecclesiastical, or of the metropolitan of this realm.

And also, that if there shall happen any contempt or irreverence to be used in the ceremonies or rites of the Church, by the misusing of the orders appointed in this book, the queen's majesty may, by the like advice of the said commissioners or metropolitan, ordain and publish such further ceremonies or rites, as may be most for the advancement of God's glory, the edifying of His Church, and the due reverence of Christ's holy mysteries and sacraments.

And be it further enacted by the authority aforesaid,

that all laws, statutes, and ordinances, wherein or whereby any other service, administration of sacraments or common prayer, is limited, established, or set forth to be used within this realm, or any other the queen's dominions or countries, shall from henceforth be utterly void and of none effect.

APPENDIX F

The CONVENTICLE ACT of 1593

For the preventing and avoiding of such great inconveniencies and perils as might happen and grow by the wicked and dangerous practices of seditious sectaries and disloyal persons; be it enacted by the Queen's most excellent majesty, and by the Lords spiritual and temporal, and the Commons, in this present Parliament assembled, and by the authority of the same, that if any person or persons above the age of sixteen years, which shall obstinately refuse to repair to some church, chapel, or usual place of common prayer, to hear divine service established by her majesty's laws and statutes in that behalf made, and shall forbear to do the same by the space of a month next after, without lawful cause, shall at any time after forty days next after the end of this session of Parliament, by printing, writing, or express words or speeches, advisedly and purposely practise or go about to move or persuade any of her majesty's subjects, or any other within her highness's realms or dominions, to deny, withstand, and impugn her majesty's power and authority in causes ecclesiastical, united, and annexed to the imperial crown of this realm; or to that end or purpose shall advisedly and maliciously move or persuade any other person whatsoever to forbear or abstain from coming to church to hear divine service, or to receive the communion according to her majesty's laws and statutes aforesaid, or to come to or be present at any unlawful assemblies, conventicles, or meetings, under colour or pretence of any exercise of religion, contrary to her majesty's said laws and statutes; or if any person or persons which shall obstinately refuse to repair to some church, chapel, or usual place of common prayer, and shall forbear by the space of a month to hear divine service, as is aforesaid, shall after the said forty days, either of him or themselves, or by the motion, persuasion, enticement, or allurement of any other, willingly join, or be present at, any such assemblies, conventicles, or meetings, under colour or pretence of any such exercise of religion, contrary to the laws and statutes of this realm, as is aforesaid; that then every such person so offending as aforesaid, and being thereof lawfully convicted, shall be committed to prison, there to remain without bail or mainprise, until they shall conform and yield themselves to come to some church, chapel, or usual place of common prayer, and hear divine service, according to her majesty's laws and statutes aforesaid, and to make such open submission and declaration of their said conformity, as hereafter in this Act is declared and appointed.

Provided always, and be it further enacted by the authority aforesaid, that if any such person or persons, which shall offend against this Act as aforesaid, shall not within three months next after they shall be convicted of their said offence, conform themselves to the obedience of the laws and statutes of this realm, in coming to the church to hear divine service, and in making such public confession and submission, as hereafter in this Act is appointed and expressed, being thereunto required by the bishop of the diocese, or any justice of the peace of the county where the same person shall happen to be, or by the minister or curate of the parish; that in every such case every such offender, being thereunto warned or required by any justice of the peace of the same county where such offender shall then be, shall upon his and their corporal oath before the justices of the peace in the open quarter sessions of the same county, or at the assizes and gaol-delivery of the same county, before the justices of the same assizes and gaol-delivery, abjure this realm of England, and all other the queen's majesty's dominions for ever, unless her majesty shall license the party to return, and thereupon shall depart out of this realm at such haven or port, and within such time, as shall in that behalf be assigned and appointed by the said justices before whom such abjuration shall be made, unless the same offender be letted or stayed by such lawful and reasonable means or causes, as by the common laws of this realm are permitted and allowed in cases of abjuration for felony; and in such cases of let or stay, then within such reasonable and convenient time after, as the common law requires in case of abjuration for felony, as is aforesaid; and that the justices of peace before whom any such abjuration shall happen to be made, as is aforesaid, shall cause the same presently to be entered of record before them, and shall certify the same to the justices of assizes and gaol-delivery of the said county, at the next assizes or gaol-delivery to be holden in the same county.

And if any such offender, which by the tenor and intent of this Act is to be abjured as is aforesaid, shall refuse to make such abjuration as is aforesaid, or after such abjuration made, shall not go to such haven, and within such time as is before appointed, and from thence depart out of this realm, according to this present Act, or after such his departure shall return or come again into any her majesty's realms or dominions, without her majesty's special licence in that behalf first had and obtained; that then, in every such case, the person so offending shall be adjudged a felon, and shall suffer as in case of felony, without benefit of clergy.

And furthermore be it enacted by the authority of this present Parliament, that if any person or persons that shall at any time hereafter offend against this Act, shall before he or they be so warned or required to make abjuration according to the tenor of this Act, repair to some parish church on some Sunday or other festival day, and then and there hear divine service, and at service-time, before the sermon, or reading of the gospel, make public and open submission and declaration of his and their conformity to her majesty's laws and statutes, as hereafter in this Act is declared and appointed; that then the same offender shall thereupon be clearly discharged of and from all and every the penalties and punishments inflicted or imposed by this Act for any of the offences aforesaid. The same submission to be made as hereafter follows, that is to say:

'I, A. B., do humbly confess and acknowledge, that I have grievously offended God in condemning her majesty's godly and lawful government and authority, by absenting myself from church, and from hearing divine service, contrary to the godly laws and statutes of this realm, and in using and frequenting disordered and unlawful conventicles and assemblies, under pretence and colour of exercise of religion: and I am heartily sorry for the same, and do acknowledge and testify in my conscience that no other person has or ought to have any power or authority over her majesty: and I do promise and protest, without any dissimulation, or any colour or means of any dispensation, that from henceforth I will from time to time obey and perform her majesty's laws and statutes, in repairing to the church and hearing divine service, and do my uttermost endeavour to maintain and defend the same.'

And that every minister or curate of every parish where such submission and declaration of conformity shall hereafter be so made by any such offender as aforesaid, shall presently enter the same into a book to be kept in every parish for that purpose, and within ten days next following shall certify the same in writing to the bishop of the same diocese.

Provided nevertheless, that if any such offender, after such submission made as is aforesaid shall afterwards fall into relapse, or eftsoons obstinately refuse to repair to some church, chapel, or usual place of common prayer, to hear divine service, and shall forbear the same as aforesaid, or shall come and be present at any such assemblies, conventicles, or meetings, under colour or pretence of any exercise of religion, contrary to her majesty's laws and statutes; that then every such offender shall lose all such benefit as he or she might otherwise by virtue of this Act have or enjoy by reason of their said submission, and shall thereupon stand and remain in such plight, condition, and degree, to all intents as though such submission had never been made.

And for that every person having house and family, is in duty bound to have special regard of the good government and ordering of the same; be it enacted by the authority aforesaid, that if any person or persons shall at any time hereafter relieve, maintain, retain, or keep in his or their house or otherwise, any person which shall obstinately refuse to come to some church, chapel, or usual place of common prayer, to hear divine service, and shall forbear the same by the space of a month together, contrary to the laws and statutes of this realm; that then every person who shall so relieve, maintain, retain, or keep any such person offending as aforesaid, after notice thereof to him or them given by the ordinary of the diocese, or any justice of assizes of the circuit, or any justice of peace of the county, or the minister, curate, or churchwardens of the parish where such person shall then be, or by any of them, shall forfeit to the queen's majesty for every person so relieved, maintained, retained, or kept, after such notice as aforesaid, ten pounds for every month that he or they shall so relieve, maintain, retain, or keep any such person so offending.

Provided nevertheless, that this Act shall not in any wise extend to punish or impeach any person or persons for relieving, maintaining, or keeping his or their wife, father, mother, child or children, ward, brother or sister, or his wife's father or mother, not having any certain place of habitation of their own, or the husbands or wives of any of them; or for relieving, maintaining, or keeping any such person as shall be committed by authority to the custody of any by whom they shall be so relieved, maintained, or kept; anything in this Act contained to the contrary notwithstanding.

And for the more speedy levying and recovering, for and by the queen's majesty, of all and singular the pains, duties, forfeitures and payments which at any time hereafter shall accrue, grow, or be payable by virtue of this Act, or of the statute made in the three and twentieth year of her majesty's reign concerning recusants; be it enacted by the authority aforesaid, that all and every the said pains, duties, forfeitures, and payments, shall and may be recovered and levied to her majesty's use, by action of debt, bill, plaint, information, or otherwise, in any of the courts commonly called the king's bench, common pleas, or exchequer, in such sort, and in all respects, as by the ordinary course of the common laws of this realm any other debt due by any such person in any other case should or may be recovered or levied, wherein no essoin, protection, or wager of law shall be admitted or allowed.

Provided always, that the third part of the penalties to be had or received by virtue of this Act, shall be employed and bestowed to such good and charitable uses, and in such manner and form, as is limited and appointed in the statute made in the twenty-eighth year of her majesty's reign touching recusants.

Provided also, that no popish recusant, or feme covert, shall be compelled or bound to abjure by virtue of this Act.

Provided also, that every person that shall abjure by force of this Act, or refuse to abjure, being thereunto required as aforesaid, shall forfeit and lose to her majesty all his goods and chattels for ever, and shall further lose all his lands, tenements, and hereditaments, for and during the life only of such offender, and no longer, and that the wife of any offender, by force of this Act, shall not lose her dower; nor that any corruption of blood shall grow or be by reason of any offence mentioned in this Act, but that the heir of every such offender, by force of this Act, shall and may, after the death of every offender, have and enjoy the lands, tenements, and hereditaments of such offender, as if this Act had not been made: and this Act to continue no longer than to the end of the next session of Parliament.

APPENDIX G

The MILLENARY PETITION (1603)

Most gracious and dread sovereign, Seeing it has pleased the Divine majesty, to the great comfort of all good Christians, to advance your highness, according to your just title, to the peaceable government of this Church and Commonwealth of England, we, the ministers of the gospel in this land, neither as factious men affecting a popular parity in the Church, nor as schismatics aiming at the dissolution of the State ecclesiastical, but as the faithful servants of Christ and loyal subjects to your majesty, desiring and longing for the redress of divers abuses of the Church, could do no less in our obedience to God, service to your majesty, love to His Church, than acquaint your princely majesty with our particular griefs; for as your princely pen writeth, 'the king, as a good physician, must first know what peccant humours his patient naturally is most subject unto, before he can begin his cure;' and although divers of us that sue for reformation have formerly, in respect of the times, subscribed to the book—some upon protestation, some upon exposition given them, some with condition rather than the Church should have been deprived of their labour and ministry—yet now we, to the number of more than a thousand of your majesty's subjects and ministers, all groaning as under a common burden of human rites and ceremonies, do with one joint consent humble ourselves at your majesty's feet, to be eased and relieved in this behalf. Our humble suit, then, unto your majesty is that these offences following, some may be removed, some amended, some qualified:

I.   In the Church service: that the cross in baptism, interrogatories ministered to infants, confirmation, as superfluous, may be taken away; baptism not to be ministered by women, and so explained; the cap and surplice not urged; that examination may go before the communion; that it be ministered with a sermon; that divers terms of priests, and absolution, and some other used, with the ring in marriage, and other such like in the book, may be corrected; the longsomeness of service abridged, Church songs and music moderated to better edification; that the Lord's Day be not profaned; the rest upon holy days not so strictly urged; that there may be a uniformity of doctrine prescribed; no popish opinion to be any more taught or defended; no ministers charged to teach their people to bow at the name of Jesus; that the canonical Scriptures only be read in the Church.

II. Concerning Church ministers: that none hereafter be admitted into the ministry but able and sufficient men, and those to preach diligently and especially upon the Lord's day; that such as be already entered and cannot preach, may either be removed, and some charitable course taken with them for their relief, or else be forced, according to the value of their livings, to maintain preachers; that non-residency be not permitted; that King Edward's statute for the lawfulness of ministers' marriages be revived; that ministers be not urged to subscribe, but according to the law, to the Articles of Religion, and the king's supremacy only.

III. For Church livings and maintenance: that bishops leave their commendams, some holding parsonages, some prebends, some vicarages, with their bishoprics; that double-beneficed men be not suffered to hold some two, some three benefices with cure, and some two, three, or four dignities besides; that impropriations annexed to bishoprics and colleges be demised only to the preachers incumbents, for the old rent; that the impropriations of laymen's fees be charged, with a sixth or seventh part of their worth, to the maintenance of the preaching minister.

IV. For Church discipline: that the discipline and excommunication may be administered according to Christ's own institution, or, at the least, that enormities may be redressed, as namely, that excommunication come not forth under the name of lay persons, chancellors, officials, &c.; that men be not excommunicated for trifles and twelve-penny matters; that none be excommunicated without consent of his pastor; that the officers be not suffered to extort unreasonable fees; that none having jurisdiction or registers' places, put out the same to farm; that divers popish canons (as for restraint of marriage at certain times) be reversed; that the longsomeness of suits in ecclesiastical courts (which hang sometimes two, three, four, five, six, or seven years) may be restrained; that the oath Ex Officio, whereby men are forced to accuse themselves, be more sparingly used; that licences for marriages without banns asked, be more cautiously granted:

These, with such other abuses yet remaining and practised in the Church of England, we are able to show not to be agreeable to the Scriptures, if it shall please your highness further to hear us, or more at large by writing to be informed, or by conference among the learned to be resolved; and yet we doubt not but that, without any further process, your majesty (of whose Christian judgment we have received so good a taste already) is able of yourself to judge of the equity of this cause. God, we trust, has appointed your highness our physician to heal these diseases; and we say with Mordecai to Esther, 'Who knoweth whether you are come to the kingdom for such a time?' Thus your majesty shall do that which we are persuaded shall be acceptable to God, honourable to your majesty in all succeeding ages, profitable to His Church, which shall be thereby increased, comfortable to your ministers, which shall be no more suspended, silenced, disgraced, imprisoned for men's traditions, and prejudicial to none but to those that seek their own quiet, credit and profit in the world.

Thus, with all dutiful submission, referring ourselves to your majesty's pleasure for your gracious answer, as God shall direct you, we most humbly recommend your highness to the Divine majesty, whom we beseech, for Christ His sake, to dispose your royal heart to do herein what shall be to His glory, the good of His Church, and your endless comfort.

Your majesty's most humble subjects, the ministers of the Gospel that desire not a disorderly innovation, but a due and godly reformation.

APPENDIX H

Historical Timeline

1507   Martin Luther is ordained as a priest at Erfurt

1509   Henry VIII becomes King of England

1509   Birth of John Calvin

1510   Luther sent to Rome on monastic business.

1513   Leo X becomes Pope

1514   Birth of John Knox

1515   While teaching on Romans, Luther realizes faith and justification are the work of God

1517   Martin Luther nails 95 Theses to the door of the church in Wittenburg.

1519   Charles V becomes Emperor of the Holy Roman Empire

1521   Martin Luther is excommunicated

1525   Luther's *The Bondage of the Will* published. Many of Luthers essays, discourses, treatises, conversations, etc. are collected in his *Table Talk*

1531   Death of Ulrich Zwingli

1534   Henry VIII declares himself "The only supreme head in earth of the Church of England" *1st Act of Supremacy*

1536   Death of Desiderius Erasmus

1536   William Tyndale strangled and burned at the stake

1536   First edition of *Calvin's Institutes* published

1543   Knox converted

1545   The Council of Trent begins

1546   Death of Martin Luther

1547   Edward VI becomes King of England

1553   Mary Tudor (Bloody Mary) begins her reign

1558   Elizabeth I crowned

1559   The *Act of Uniformity* requires use of 1559 *Book of Common Prayer*; 2nd *Act of Supremacy* instated under Queen Elizabeth I

1560   Birth of Jacobus Arminius

1560   1st Publication of Geneva Bible

1560   Parliament approves the *Scot's Confession*, penned by the six Johns

1563   The Council of Trent concludes

1564   Death of John Calvin

1566   Bullinger writes *The Second Helvetic Confession*

1567-1568   The Vestments Controversy

1571   Thirty Nine Articles are finalized

1572   Death of John Knox

1572   Massacre of St. Bartholomew's Day–persecution of Huguenots

1590   Thomas Cartwright and others arrested

1593   Birth of George Herbert

1593   The Conventicle Act of 1593 is enacted, forbidding private worship and requiring attendance at the established church on pain of imprisonment, exile, and even death, absent conformity.

1596   Birth of Moses Amyrald, founder of Amyraldianism

1596   Birth of Rene Descartes, founder of rationalism

1598   Edict of Nantes grants Huguenots greater religious freedom

1599   The 1599 Edition of the Geneva Bible published

1603   Arminius states position on predestination

1603   James VI of Scotland becomes James I of England

1603   A thousand Puritan ministers sign the Millenary Petition, calling for King James to conform Church ceremonies and practices to the Word of God

1604   King James confers with Puritan leaders at Hampton Court, rejecting the Millinary Petition, declaring, *"I will make them conform, or I will harry them out of the land."*

1608   Puritan separatists from town of Scrooby migrate to Netherlands to avoid persecution

1609   Death of Jacobus Arminius

1611   The King James Version of the Bible published

1615   Birth of Puritan Richard Baxter, author of *The Reformed Pastor*

1616   Birth of Puritan John Owen

1618-1619   The Synod of Dort responds to Arminianism

1620   Scrooby Separatists return to England and sail for Virginia on the Mayflower; Plymouth, Massachusetts colony founded

1623   Birth of Blaise Pascal

1623   Birth of Francis Turretin

1625   Charles I becomes King

1628   William Laud becomes Bishop of London

1628   Birth of Puritan John Bunyan, author of *Pilgrim's Progress*

1629   Charles I dismisses Parliament

1630   John Winthrop and many Puritans migrate to America

1632   Birth of John Locke, founder of Empiricism

1635 Roger Williams banished from Bay Colony; founds Providence the following year

1636 Harvard founded by Puritans

1637 Native Americans and Puritans battle in Pequot War; New Haven colony founded

1638 Anne Hutchinson banished

1638 The National Covenant (Scotland)

1643 The Solemn League and Covenant (Scotland)

1643-1646 The Westminster Assembly meets

1646 Cromwell's army defeats the King's army at the Battle of Naseby

1647 George Fox founds the Religious Society of Friends (Quakers)

1649 Charles I is executed; Oliver Cromwell becomes Lord Protector

1658 Death of Oliver Cromwell

AUTHORITIES

Dangerous Positions published and practised within this Iland of Brytaine under pretence of Reformation. 1593.

A Survey of the Pretended Holy Discipline. 1593.

The Perpetual Government of Christes Church by Thos. Bilson, Warden of Winchester College. 1593.

A Parte of a Register, *The State of the Church of England laid open in a Conference.*

Life of John Whitgift by Sir George Paule. 1599.

Sir Simonds D'Ewes' Journal of Parliament in the Reign of Queen Elizabeth. 1693.

The Presbyterian Movement in the Reign of Queen Elizabeth as illustrated by the Minute Book of the Dedham Classes, 1582—1589. R. Hist. Soc. 1905.

Strype's Lives: Archbishop Parker, 1711; Archbishop Grindal, 1710; Archbishop Whitgift, 1718. 3 vols. folia.

Strype's Annals. 4 vols. folio. 1735.

Neal's *History of the Puritans*, 1732—1738.

A Retrospect of Religious Life in England by J. J. Tayler.1853.

History of the Early Puritans by J. B. Marsden. 1854.

History of the Church of England by R. W. Dixon. 6 vols. 1878—1902.

Introduction to the Fifth Book of *Hooker's Ecclesiastical Polity*— the Puritan Position, by Francis Paget, D.D. 1899.

Church and State under the Tudors, by Gilbert W. Child, of Exeter College, Oxford.1890.

Oliver Cromwell and the Rule of the Puritans in England by Charles Firth, M.A. 1903.

Carlyle's *Letters and Speeches of Oliver Cromwell.* 1904.

AUTHORITIES

History of the English Church during the Civil Wars and under the Commonwealth, 1640—1660, by W. A. Shaw, Litt.D. 2 vols. 1900.

Henry Barrow, Separatist (1550 — 1593), by Fred. J. Powicke, Ph.D. 1900.

The Martin Marprelate Tracts. W. Pierce, 1909.

History of the University of Cambridge, by J. Bass Mullinger. 1888.

State Papers, Domestic, Elizabeth, James I…Charles I.

Zurich Letters, 1558—1579; Second Series, 1558—1602. Parker Society.

Documents Illustrative of English Church History. Edited by Henry Gee and W. J. Harding, 1896.

ENDNOTES

1. *History of England*, 1863, quoted by Maurice Ashley in *The Greatness of Oliver Cromwell* (London: Hodder & Stoughton, 1957), p. 14. Hereafter cited as "Ashley."

2. Ashley, p. 18.

3. *Ibid.*

4. J.H Merle D'Aubigne, *The Protector* (Harrisonburg, VA: Sprinkle Publications, 1997), p. 230. Hereafter cited as "*The Protector.*"

5. Otto Scott, *The Great Christian Revolution* (Windsor, NY: Reformer Library, 1994), p. 128. Hereafter cited as "Scott."

6. *Ibid.*, p. 191.

7.   Alexander Mitchell, *The Westminster Assembly: Its History and Standards* (Canada: Still Waters Revival Books, [1883] 1992, printed in the United States of America), p. 81.

8.   William Maxwell Hetherington, *The History of the Westminster Assembly of Divines* (Edmonton, AB Canada: Still Waters Revival Books, [1856] 1993), p. 71.

9.   J.I. Packer, *A Quest for Godliness*, (Wheaton, IL: Crossway Books, 1990), p. 28. Hereafter cited as "Packer."

10.   *Ibid.*

11.   *Journal of Christian Reconstruction,* Winter 1979-80, p. 3.

12.   *The Protector,* pp. 30, 34.

13.   *Ibid,* p. 58.

14.   *Ibid.,* p. 59-60.

15.   Memoirs of Sir Philip Warwick (London, 1701), p. 247, as quoted in *The Protector,* p. 35.

16.   *The Protector,* pp. 44, 46.

17.   Scott, p. 245.

18.   As cited by Scott, p. 245.

19.   *The Protector,* p. 50.

20.   *Ibid.,* pp. 50-51.

21.   Scott, p. 260.

22.   *Ibid.,* p. 261.

23.   *The Protector,* p. 82.

24. *The Protector*, p. 84.

25. Scott, p. 266. During the restoration of the Stuart monarchy following Cromwell's death, firm evidence came to light revealing the treasonous and perfidious conspiracies. Charles I had raised an army of 10,000 men from Ireland which would combine with another army of 10,000 from the Pope and Catholic kings in Europe, which would establish Charles' tyranny at the price of an agreement with the pope to legalize Roman Catholicism in England.

26. Scott, p. 270.

27. *Ibid.*

28. *The Protector*, p. 102.

29. *The Protector*, pp. 102–104.

30. *Ibid.*, pp. 105-106.

31. *Ibid.*, p. 106.

32. *Ibid.*, p. 111.

33. Tom Reilly, *Cromwell: An Honorable Enemy* (London: Brandon Books, 1999), p. 4.

34. *The Protector*, p. 112.

35. *Ibid.*, p. 128.

36. *The Protector*, pp. 130, 140, 141.

37. As recorded in *The Protector*, p. 147.

38. *Ibid.*

39. *Ibid.*

40. Ashley, p. 278.

41. *Ibid.,* p 277.

42. *The Protector,* p. 215.

43. *The Protector,* p. 217.

44. As recorded in *The Protector,* p. 218.

45. *Ibid.,* pp. 218-219.

46. *Ibid.,* p. 220.

47. *Ibid.*

48. *Ibid.,* p. 223.

49. *Ibid.,* pp. 226-230.

50. *Ibid.,* pp. 84-85.

51. *Ibid.,* p. 266.

52. As recorded in Cromwell's *Letters and Speeches,* as cited in *The Protector,* pp. 262-63.

INDEX

A

B

U

Udall, John, 113, 115, 118, 119

Uniformity, Act of, 30, 32, 33, 34, 38, 39, 40, 81, 96

University Press. *See* Cambridge University Press

V

Vestiarian Controversy, 42

W

Waldegrave Press, 113, 115, 116

Wentworth, Peter, 72, 75

Whitgift, Archbishop, 18, 50, 56, 69, 71, 78, 79, 91, 92, 102, 105, 117, 121, 127, 135

Whittingham, Dean, 74, 220

Withers, George, 54

Wolsey, Cardinal, 54, 92